Food Art

Garnishing Made Easy.

Created by renowned Chef Gardé Mangér

John Gargone

4880 Lower Valley Road, Atglen, PA 19310 USA

Dedication

Dedicated to all of my professional colleagues, family, friends, and my faithful dog Rocko.

Acknowledgment

A special Thank You to Linda Smiley. Acknowledgment to Split Rock Resort

Library of Congress Cataloging-in-Publication Data

Gargone, John.
  Food Art : garnishing made easy / by John Gargone.
    p. cm.
  ISBN 0-7643-1960-4 (pbk.)
1. Garnishes (Cookery) 2. Vegetable carving. 3. Fruit carving.
4. Large type books. I. Title.
TX740.5 .G35 2004
641.8'19--dc22

2003018724

Designed by Mark David Bowyer
Type set in Zapf Chancery Bd BT/Humanist 521 BT

ISBN: 0-7643-1960-4
Printed in China

Published by Schiffer Publishing Ltd.
4880 Lower Valley Road
Atglen, PA 19310
Phone: (610) 593-1777; Fax: (610) 593-2002
E-mail: Info@schifferbooks.com
Please visit our web site catalog at
www.schifferbooks.com

This book may be purchased from the publisher.
Include $3.95 for shipping. Please try your bookstore first.
We are always looking for people to write books on new and related subjects. If you have an idea for a book please contact us at the above address.
You may write for a free catalog.

In Europe, Schiffer books are distributed by
Bushwood Books
6 Marksbury Avenue
Kew Gardens
Surrey TW9 4JF England
Phone: 44 (0) 20-8392-8585; Fax: 44 (0) 20-8392-9876
E-mail: info@bushwoodbooks.co.uk
Free postage in the UK. Europe: air mail at cost.

Contents

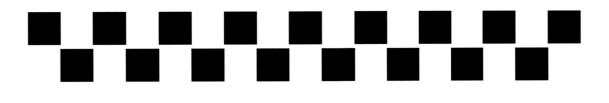

Foreword
Learn the Secrets of the Great Chefs!

We spend millions of dollars a year on vacationing and what do we always talk about upon our return? The food, the restaurants' gourmet delights or the casinos' and cruise liners' fantastic buffet displays. Sunday brunch is a big hit across the country, why? The beautiful "buffet presentations." More and more people are entertaining at home. Impress your guests and show them how much you care.

Food is like all of the colors of the painter's pallet and all the sculpture mediums combined; there is absolutely no limit as to what can be created.

In this book you will find easy to follow, fully illustrated instructions with over three hundred color photographs teaching the home entertainer as well as the professional chef a unique, systematic approach to create thousands of different edible art presentations. The techniques shown encompass all edible products, cuisines, and cultures. Learn professional knife skills, and how to personalize any event by creating unlimited theme designs easily and comfortably. Astound your guests, the food will be the hit of any event with these truly amazing and innovative methods to decorate every-day common market products. No more decorating salads with lettuce or taking all day to roll deli meat, and you won't have to hire a caterer to make your cold food displays anymore. Food is for the body, but good food presented well feeds the soul and all the senses. Show the people around you how much you care through food presentation.

Introduction to Food Garnishing

In this book you will find easy to follow instructions to create true edible art. With this unique systematic approach you will be able to create thousands of different presentations that encompass all cuisines and cultures. These methods will allow you to personalize any event and create many theme designs easily and comfortably. In all food preparation, knife skills are a tremendous asset to have. Cooking for two or two thousand, you will work safer, faster, and be more confident in your skills when you learn the knife techniques presented here. Most of the work can be done with only two sharp knives and no special gadgets.

In creating a platter or table display, there should be a focal point with height and/or distinction. The focal point can be the main ingredient, centerpiece or an arrangement of products/garnishes. If serving to only one side, the centerpiece is usually located in the back of the platter or table. The food should always be easily accessible. The whole idea behind garnishing is to enhance the main product in appearance as well as taste. To accomplish this, place the centerpiece, and/or main product, at its ideal location. From there build your design around the product; you do not have to cover the entire surface. Wipe clean any surface that is exposed.

Food can be presented on many different types of platters. Try putting the tuna or potato salad on a flat, square platter. Mirrors are great for displaying canapés, fruit, vegetable, cheese, and so much more. There are mirrors made for this or you can use the one on your wall; but, you should seal it with silicon first. Clear glass with no border is great, just place it on a black cloth and see how the food stands out. Simulated or real marble slabs, clay tiles, and even wood planks are all creative bases. Whatever you choose it must have a flat surface so food will sit evenly.

To arrange food neatly, first it must be prepared neatly. Never lay out products horizontally or vertically on a tray, always arrange them at an angle. With canapés especially, do not mix up types—lay out the same flavors in each row, alternating rows. Use a guide to cut perfect lines: ruler for straight, an upside down round or oval bowl or plate to create curved designs. Place the ruler, bowl or plate in position, lay food against the edge, and remove. All the information is in this book to create astounding and easy edible art.

Rules to Garnish By

1. Consistency is the key; always lay out products on platters in a uniform manner.
2. Cut all products in a uniform size without disturbing the order in which they are cut.
3. Lay out a sliced product in the same order as it was sliced; if it doesn't look good, don't use it.
4. When doing repetitious circular cutting, turn the product and the tool.
5. Instead of coordinating colors, contrast them, put green next to red and so on.
6. Over decorating is as bad as no decoration.
7. Garnishing should enhance the main product's appearance, not cover it up.
8. The garnish should be able to be eaten with the main product without a conflict in taste.
9. Quality garnishing starts with quality, buy the best products you can find and treat them with care.

Relax and enjoy this excellent medium for artistic self expression.

People Eat with Their Eyes Before They Eat with Their Mouths

Presentation is singularly important to serving excellent food. Sight is the first sense stimulated in the presence of a meal. From first glimpse, we develop an idea of how food should taste. Presented well, we draw positive conclusions about a food's taste at first sight. In the mind's taste bud, the food tastes even better because it looks appetizing and is relished by your guests before it is even tasted.

Consuming an artistically presented platter of food is almost a spiritual experience. After all, the meal was prepared with a great amount of consideration and enlightenment. To create such a masterpiece, a part of the creative cook remains in every bite. On many occasions Chef John would prepare unusual cold specialties such as Breast of Veal Galantine wrapped in pork caul with fresh truffles, pistachios, and coated with a burgundy choid froid or a fresh creamy scallop mousse wrapped in knori and spinach pasta sheets for an exclusive Country Club brunch in California. Without even a clue as to what they were eating, children as young as seven years old would come back for seconds; they paid the highest complement a Chef can receive.

True Chefs have a passion to extend themselves through food. After many years of searching, perfecting and simplifying techniques, Chef John has created an approach to food decorating that can be enjoyed by everyone. From the most experienced Chef to the average home cook who wants to impress, these methods are designed to be cost effective and can be applied in every day use. Anyone can learn these skills.

Show the people in your life how much you care through Food Garnishing!

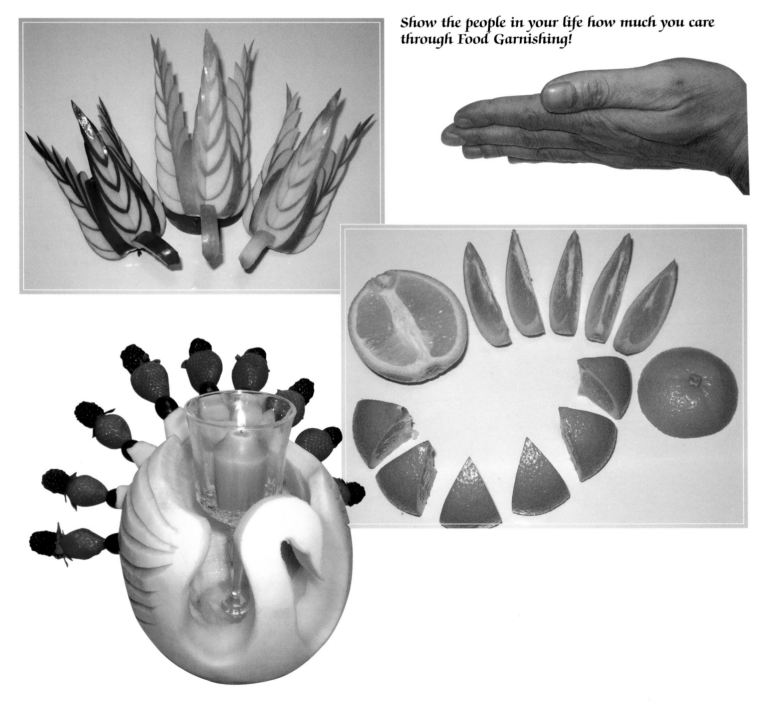

Knife Handling Techniques

Tools of the Trade

1. Sharpening stone: Water or oil with a coarse and fine grit.
2. Core tool with plunger:
    Used to core fruit; plunger will push out the core.
3. Honing Steel: Grinds a fine edge on the blade.
4. French knife: eight or ten inches in length, any quality brand.
5. Vegetable knife: Carving fruits and vegetables.
6. Paring knife: Paring and carving fruits and vegetables.

7. Parisian scoop: Scoops balls from fruit, vegetables, and potatoes.
8. Channel knife: Cuts channels one quarter inch wide.
9. Potato peeler: Peels uniform strips.
10. Daisy cutter: Sold as a cookie cutter, 2 inch.
11. Star and straight tip pastry tube.
12. Wood skewers and square picks.

Knife Sharpening

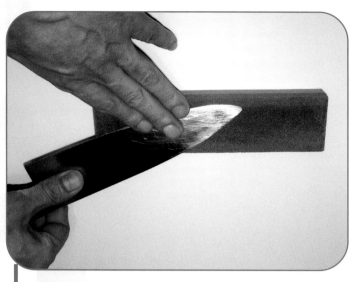

1. Adjust the angle of the knife and lock your wrist.

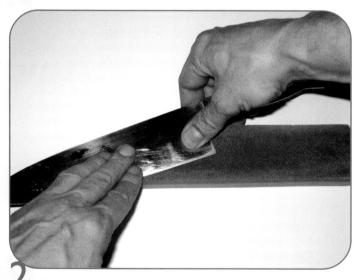

2. Slide the blade up and down the stone.

3. Repeat the process on the fine grit side of the stone.

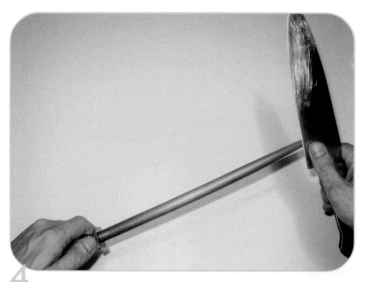

4. Hold the steel firmly in position.

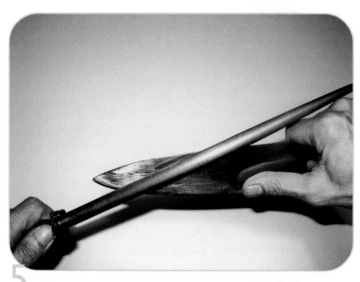

5. Using only your wrist, draw the blade down the steel and up the inside.

6. Repeat the process, continuing to keep the blade angle in position.

7. Compare blades, the machined edge is the one with a beveled edge.

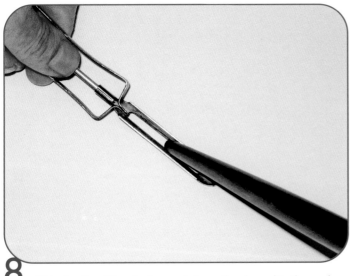

8. Slide the tip of the steel up and down the channel in the peeler.

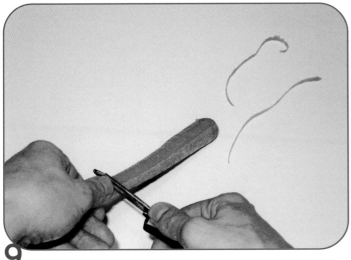

9. Peel carrots in one long stroke while turning with the other hand.

About Knives

Knife skills are key to being an efficient cook. The first thing that must be remembered is to always respect the knife. Never talk and cut, if you are distracted or approached by someone, put the knife down. Try not to cook and chop. Do all the cutting then do all the cooking. Wrap sharp knives and any special tools in a towel or a sheath and store properly. When purchasing knives, look for a well-balanced knife with a hard stainless steel blade that goes through the handle and has a gradually formed edge. Most knives have a honed V edge which interferes with the knife's performance, **see fig. 7**. The edge may be sharp, but it will be hard to control because the V pulls the knife to the side and splits the food before it cuts it. A gradually honed smooth edge is necessary for proper control and a longer edge life. Serrated knives tend to tear the product. A sharp knife is safer than a dull one.

About Knife Sharpening

A razor sharp and smooth edge can be achieved with an oil or water stone. Sharpen first on the coarse side of the stone, keeping the stone wet at all times. Lay the blade flat on the side and apply pressure on the edge to get the correct angle, **see fig. 1**. Keep tilted to that angle and slide the knife up and down the stone while pushing down firmly. Continue until all of the original V edge is gone, turn the knife over and finish the other side, **see fig. 2**. When the V edge is gone on both sides, turn the stone over to fine grit and continue to sharpen, **see fig. 3**. Repeat the process while checking the sharpness; the first sharpening is the most difficult. Never cut on a plate, metal, tile or anything but a cutting board or the knife will be damaged.

Steeling the Knife

After sharpening on the stone there will still be tiny burrs on the edge. Check for burrs by carefully sliding a finger on the side of the edge. These burrs will drag the blade when cutting and dull the knife prematurely. To remove those burrs and restore the edge after periodic use or a fresh sharpening, finish the edge on a steel to get a smooth razors edge. Holding the steel in an upright locked position in one hand and the knife in the other, lay the blade flat on the steel. Using only the wrist slide the knife down the outside of the steel and up the inside. Repeat. Following this method can produce a razor sharp edge that will last, **see fig. 4, 5 and 6**.

About Vegetable Peelers

There are many shapes and sizes, some cut thick and some cut thin. I have always preferred the standard; a quality basic stainless steel peeler. Unfortunately you will not know the thickness a peeler will cut until you try it. A good

peeler should be able to take off a long thin strip of carrot without breaking. The strip should be about the thickness of a piece of paper. To peel a carrot efficiently, **see fig. 9**. Hold a carrot by the tip and put the bottom on a table. Start at the tip and in one motion peel the length of the carrot, letting the peeler hit the table. Turn the carrot, not the peeler, and continue until you have a smooth, round carrot; after all of the carrots are peeled then trim all the ends to save time.

Sharpening Peelers

To sharpen a peeler, turn it upside down and hold in place on the work surface. Gently push the tip of sharpening steel up and down between the blades, **see fig. 8**. Always clean the peeler immediately after use; starch will ruin the blades.

Knife Grip

Cutting any vegetable is easy if you follow a few precautions. To hold the blade correctly:

Grasp the very bottom of the blade with your thumb and forefinger, **see fig. 1**.

Wrap your three fingers around the handle to get a secure and comfortable grip, **see fig. 2**.

To slice something large, use a sharp slicing knife or a good French knife. Move the knife back and forth, like you would a saw, while putting only a small amount of downward pressure on the knife. Let the knife do the cutting and keep your wrists locked. If you're slicing something small keep the handle pointed up and the tip down. With one motion pull the knife down and back.

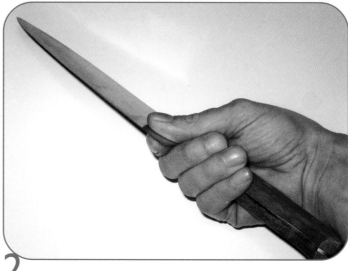

2. Wrap three fingers securely around the handle.

Professional Slicing Techniques

Curl your fingers back while holding the product, **see fig. 3, 4, 5, 6**.

Position the index finger's lower knuckle so it is protruding slightly to guide the blade.

Position the blade and tilt it slightly away from your other hand.

Put the index finger's lower knuckle against the blade.

Lock those wrists and concentrate on what you are doing.

Draw the knife to start the cut.

If you are cutting something large, like a watermelon, or slicing something delicate, like a side of smoked salmon, or something difficult, like a pineapple, jig the knife.

While putting only a slight pressure on the knife, jig the knife back and forth quickly.

While lifting the blade from the completed cut the other hand is repositioning.

Once you learn this technique you will be slicing and chopping with the best of them.

To cut hard cheese, rock the knife instead of sawing.

For slicing something like a cucumber, position the knife so the handle is pointing at 2:00.

Draw the blade down and slightly back.

Reposition the left guide finger while bringing the blade up.

Reposition the blade against guide finger.

Repeat slowly, in time you will naturally go faster.

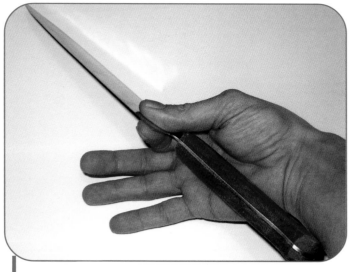

1. Position the blade as shown.

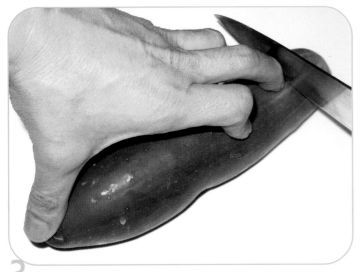

3. Position both hands correctly and angle the blade.

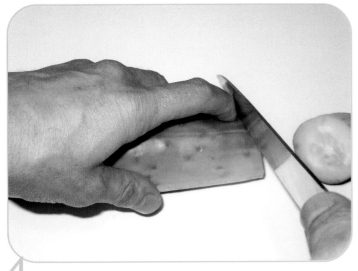

4. Keep the handle up and the tip pointed down.

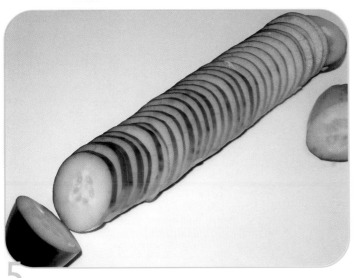

5. This was sliced blindfolded in four seconds, it's not magic, just practice.

6. Use your thumb to pull the guide fingers back while slicing even the smallest product.

On The Bias

Bias Cutting means to cut at an angle, the more of an angle, the longer the slice.

Always use the other hand to guide the thickness of the cut, **see fig. 1**.

Keep the blade pointed down with the handle up; this will prevent the slices from sticking to the blade.

Cut slices in even thickness for the best presentation effect, **see fig. 2**.

2. Hold the celery rib on its side for bias slices.

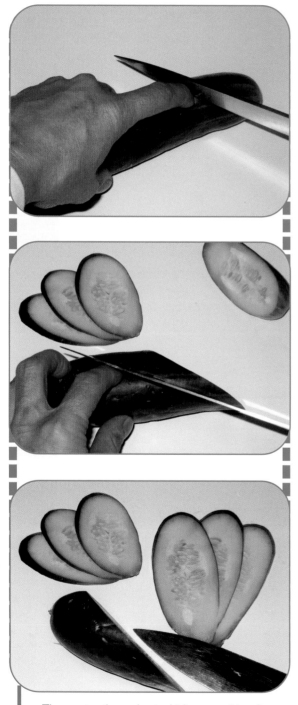

Dicing Vegetables

First you have to cut vegetables into strips; the thickness will depend on the size of dice, see **figures 3, 4, 5.**

1. The greater the angle at which you position the blade, the longer the slices will be.

3. Cut celery ribs into the proper thickness. For a small dice cut, the strips are about a quarter inch, for a bigger dice, cut the strips accordingly, then cross cut for a dice.

4. Leave the core intact to hold the slices together.

6. Cut a third slice off the bottom of the orange so it sits flat.

5. Cross cut for a fine dice. No need to cut horizontally.

Wedge Cutting Technique

Oranges for example can be cut into four to twenty four wedges depending on the size of the garnish.

Cut off the bottom of the orange and then carefully cut in a star pattern, **see fig. 6, 7**.

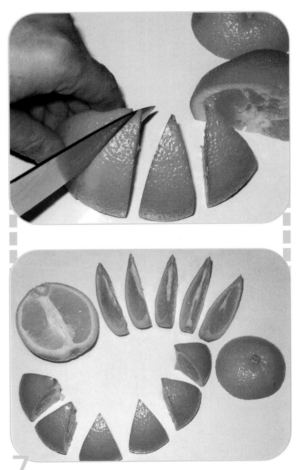

7. Split the orange into two halves, cut each half as shown. Hold the side while cutting so the delicate bottom is not crushed.

8. Stand the wedges on the flat end and arrange. Use any form for a template. Pull it away when the pattern is complete.

The half wedges should stand up on the flat end and can be arranged to create patterns, salad borders or to hold individual and buffet portions of food, **see fig. 8, 9**.

9. Fill with cut fruit or berries; use your imagination.

To make wedges for garnish, always cut through the center to achieve uniformity.

Salad Border Garnishing

Technique

Uses: Bowl and Platter Garnishing, Food Holders and Salad Borders
Tools: Sharp paring knife, sharp French knife, and a good potato peeler

Tricks of the Trade

For salad border garnishing you only need to master two basic cuts, slices and wedges. From these two basic cuts there are endless variations. From the basic designs illustrated here, many elaborate variations can be easily created.

Method 1

1. Arrange any salad on a platter or bowl; use a spatula to form a smooth, mounded surface.
2. Clean the rim of the bowl or platter carefully with a paper towel.
3. Pick out a nice straight, fat cucumber with a deep green color or a zucchini or a . . .
4. Cut a thin slice off the side so cucumber lays flat on the table and the rim of the salad.
5. Keeping the handle up and the point down on the knife, slice quarter inch even slices.
6. Like a deck of cards pick up a stack of slices and lay them around the rim of the bowl or platter.

Tip:

Lay the slices out the same way they come off the cucumber (do not mix them up). Arrange slices end to end until you reach the first slice to complete a continuous chain.

7. Slice some cherry tomatoes or black olives directly in half through the stem end.
8. Place the halved tomato, with the flat side covering where the cucumber slices meet. Continue placing the tomato halves on the cucumber slices to seal all the seams and create a continuous chain.

Method 2

1. Put any salad on a platter or bowl; use a spatula to form a smooth, mounded surface.
2. Clean the rim carefully with a paper towel.
3. Pick out a few tomatoes that are the same size, with a good color and even roundness.
4. Cut tomatoes in half through the core then cut each half into 3 equal wedges.
5. Cut about 4 extra large black olives in half through pitted end and quarter.
6. Place tomato wedge side down against the rim of your platter and gently push down a little.
7. Place second tomato wedge next to the first with the core ends all pointing the same way following the platter or bowl rim, continue until you meet the first wedge.
8. Place each black olive wedge, smooth side up between each tomato wedge. This will give the appearance of a continuous chain by hiding the seams of the tomato chain.

The variations are as endless as the produce market and your imagination.

Creamy Carrot Raisin Slaw

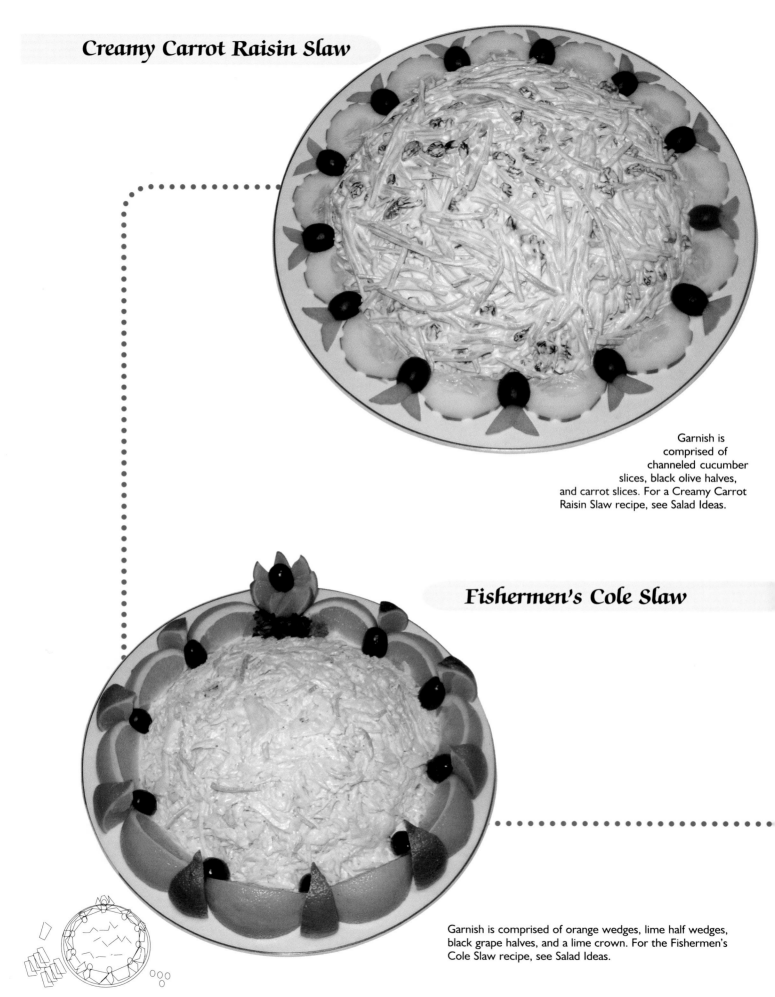

Garnish is comprised of channeled cucumber slices, black olive halves, and carrot slices. For a Creamy Carrot Raisin Slaw recipe, see Salad Ideas.

Fishermen's Cole Slaw

Garnish is comprised of orange wedges, lime half wedges, black grape halves, and a lime crown. For the Fishermen's Cole Slaw recipe, see Salad Ideas.

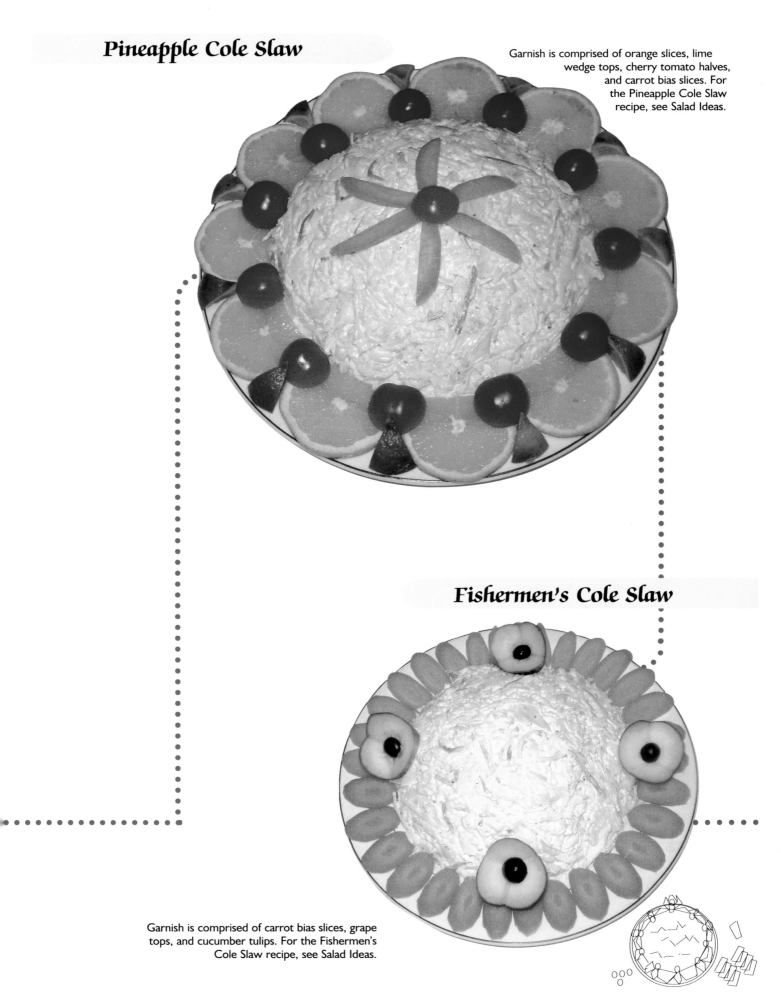

Pineapple Cole Slaw

Garnish is comprised of orange slices, lime wedge tops, cherry tomato halves, and carrot bias slices. For the Pineapple Cole Slaw recipe, see Salad Ideas.

Fishermen's Cole Slaw

Garnish is comprised of carrot bias slices, grape tops, and cucumber tulips. For the Fishermen's Cole Slaw recipe, see Salad Ideas.

Angel Hair Basil Pesto

Garnish is comprised of cherry tomato halves and black olive wedges. For the Angel Hair Basil Pesto recipe, see Salad Ideas.

Spanish Sausage Salad

Garnish is comprised of bias cut cucumbers, carrots, and a yellow squash Tulip. For the Spanish Sausage Salad recipe, see Salad Ideas.

Beef and Black Olive Salad

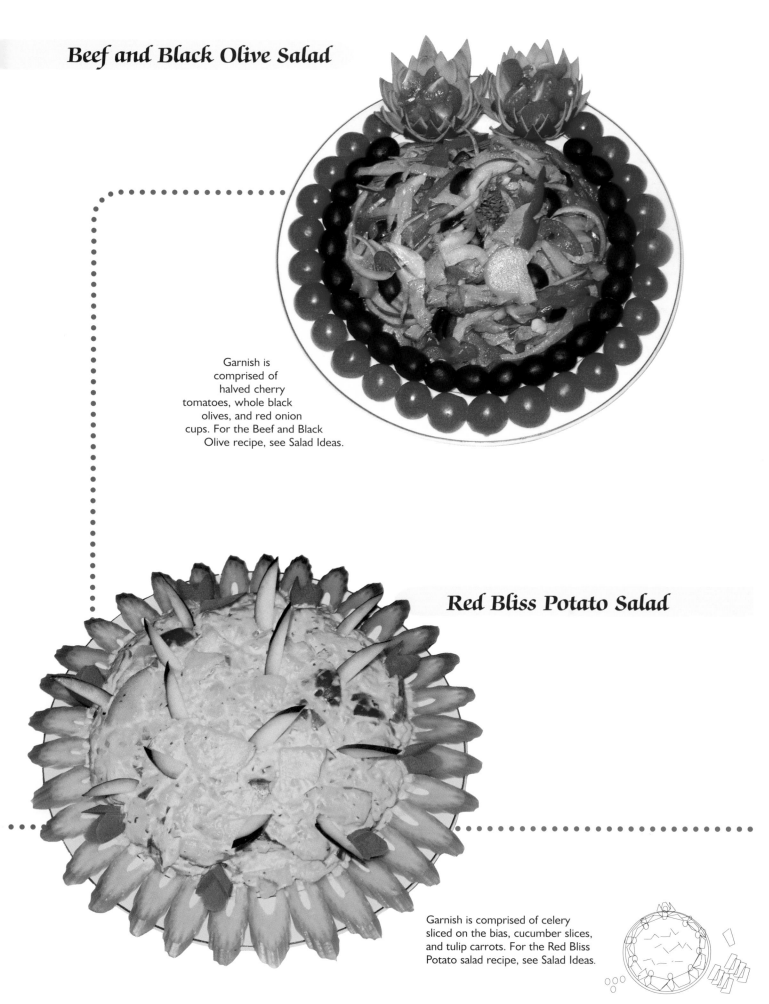

Garnish is comprised of halved cherry tomatoes, whole black olives, and red onion cups. For the Beef and Black Olive recipe, see Salad Ideas.

Red Bliss Potato Salad

Garnish is comprised of celery sliced on the bias, cucumber slices, and tulip carrots. For the Red Bliss Potato salad recipe, see Salad Ideas.

Marinated Chic Pea

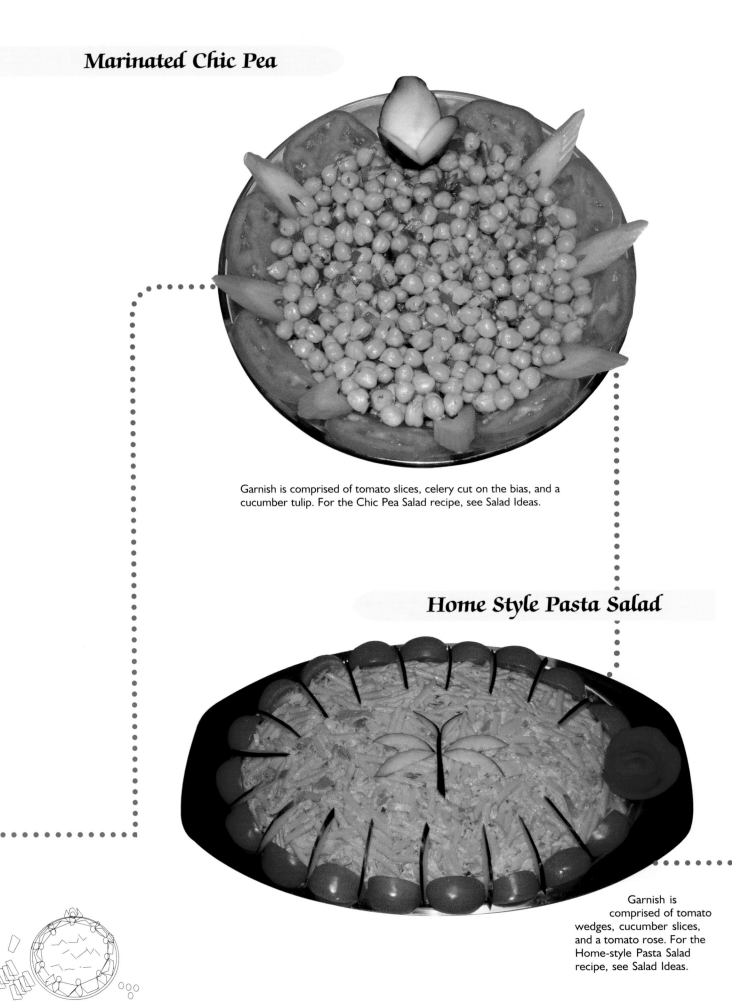

Garnish is comprised of tomato slices, celery cut on the bias, and a cucumber tulip. For the Chic Pea Salad recipe, see Salad Ideas.

Home Style Pasta Salad

Garnish is comprised of tomato wedges, cucumber slices, and a tomato rose. For the Home-style Pasta Salad recipe, see Salad Ideas.

Favorite Salad Recipes

Tricks of the Trade

Add pasta or potatoes to boiling salted water. After it reaches a second boil, turn potatoes for even cooking. Pastas must be vigorously moved around for the first five minutes to prevent sticking. Cook the potatoes until fork tender. Both should be shocked in cold water and stored dry in the cooler until well chilled. Do not add mayonnaise to a salad that is above forty-five degrees. Always prepare your salads twenty-four hours in advance so flavors blend correctly.

Red Bliss Potato Salad
3 pounds of tiny red potatoes boiled and quartered and chilled.
1/4 pound of bacon sautéed slowly to a crisp with fat, add while warm.
1 large leek top steamed and diced medium size.
5 boiled eggs will be squished into chunks.
1-1/2 cups of celery chopped medium to fine in the food processor.
In a separate bowl blend: 1 cup of sour cream, 1/4 cup yellow mustard, 1 cup mayonnaise, a couple jigs of Worcestershire and tabasco.
Add 2 teaspoons of salt and 1 teaspoon of celery salt and black pepper.
Blend all except potatoes, add potatoes last on top of blend and fold.

Picnic style Macaroni Salad
2 pounds macaroni cooked al dente and chilled.
Dice small 1/4 pound of ham and 1/4 pound sharp yellow cheddar.
Dice small 1 stalk celery, 2 red and 2 green peppers, and 2 medium carrots.
Bind all with mayonnaise, salt & pepper, and a couple jigs of Worcestershire and a drop of tabasco.

Fisherman's Cole Slaw
Shred 1 head each of red and white cabbage.
Dressing: Mix 6 Tblsp sugar with 3 oz. cider vinegar.
Blend with 1 cup mayonnaise.
Add lots of celery salt to taste.
Diced pineapple and shredded carrots are optional.

Creamy Carrot Raisin Slaw
1-1/2 cups shredded carrots, 1/4 cup raisins, 1/4 cup sour cream, and 2 tablespoons mayonnaise, 1 ounce cider vinegar, and 1 tablespoon sugar.

Specialty Salad Recipes

Beef and Black Olive Salad
Cut into strips about 2-inches-by-1/2-inch wide any left over roast beef.
Add halved black olives and a little olive juice, julienne of red onion, and red, green, and yellow pepper strips.
Add a little wine vinegar, olive oil, dijon mustard, and Worcestershire, season with fresh ground black pepper, sea salt, basil, and granulated garlic.

Harvard Beet Salad
Drain canned beet balls or slices and reserve 1 quart of juice.
Add 1 cup pineapple juice and 1/2 cinnamon stick and boil.
Add a fine julienne of the zest of 1 orange and 1 lemon.
Boil 2 minutes and thicken with a cornstarch or arrowroot paste.
Pour over beets while still hot and serve or chill well and serve cold.

Ambrosia Salad
Blend an array of fresh seasonal fruits, maraschino cherries, tiny marshmallows, and walnuts.
Bind with equal parts of sour cream and sweetened whip cream.
Top with toasted coconut.

Spanish Sausage Salad
Slice 1/4-inch slices of any type sausage.
Cut thin strips of green and yellow bell peppers.
Slice thin white onions and smash a little garlic.
Add chunked canned whole Italian tomatoes with juice and a little olive oil, season with sea salt, cumin's, chili powder, and granulated garlic to taste.

Rice and Smoked Lox Salad
Rice is very starchy and requires a quick chill after it is cooked.
Use any leftover rice and blend with any smoked fish.
Add your favorite fine-diced vegetables.
Add equal parts of mayonnaise and sour cream to create a moist salad.
Season with sea salt, and Worcestershire sauce.
Add white pepper until you taste the flavor change.

Mulligatawny Pasta Salad
Cooked al dente and chill fettuccini pasta.
Use the same curried paste recipe as the curried chicken salad.
Add paste a little at a time to 2 parts mayonnaise and 1 part sour cream.
Bind with pasta, adjust seasoning, and serve immediately.

Seafood Salad

Tiny cooked shrimp or crab or sea legs, imitation crabmeat.

Drain well and blend with green peppers, celery, and onion.

Use lots of vegetables, put them in a food processor, and pulse fine.

Bind with mayonnaise and season with sea salt and Worcestershire.

The key to this dish is adding white pepper to enhance the seafood flavor.

Curried Chicken, Apple, Raisin, and Date Salad

Cooked diced or pulled chicken meat.

Dice small dates, raisins, Granny smith apples, celery, and green bell pepper.

Heat sauté pan, blend salad oil and curry to make a paste.

Add brown sugar to paste to mildly sweeten and sauté for only a minute or two.

Add paste a little at a time to mayonnaise and sour cream base until desired flavor is achieved.

Season the base with salt, Worcestershire, and a little fruit chutney if desired.

Angel Hair Basil Pasta

Cooked al dente and chilled angel hair pasta dry.

Pesto: Trim and chop coarse 1 packed cup each fresh basil and parsley leaves.

Put in a food processor with kosher salt and fresh ground black pepper, 1 clove of smashed fresh garlic, and pulse until it won't chop any finer.

Add a little oil at a time to form a moveable paste and process for 5 minutes or until smooth. (Key: then add 1 tsp. white vinegar or more to enhance basil flavor. Cold salads: add a little oil to paste and blend with pasta and serve. Hot dish: add olive oil to sauté 1 Tblsp pesto for 1 serving and then toss pasta. Note: This is a potent flavor, use very little at a time until desired flavor is achieved. Adjust salt, pepper, and garlic after pasta is tossed in pesto.)

Marinated Mushrooms

Pick out the smallest and freshest button mushrooms.

Marinate in French dressing for at least two days.

Note: always wash produce by floating it in water and pulling the product out to drain.

Mushrooms Marinara

Pick out the smallest and freshest button mushrooms.

Heat a heavy bottom saucepan with olive oil.

Chop fine, then sauté lots of fresh shallots, garlic, and lots of thyme for 2 minutes. Then add mushrooms and continue to sauté for 5 minutes.

Add lots of sweet white wine and reduce by half.

Add tomato paste and more sweet white wine to desired consistency.

Simmer for 1 hour, serve hot or well chilled.

Fresh Vegetable Salad

Slice thin some broccoli, cauliflower, carrots, and celery on the bias. As a variation, try thinly sliced red onions, bell peppers, hicama, and diacon radish.

Marinate with a little white vinegar and olive oil in a covered bowl.

Do not season. … Taste it tomorrow.

Garbanzo Bean Salad

Chic peas are the same as garbanzo beans. Open can, drain well, and rinse.

Dice fine red onion, red, yellow, and green bell peppers, and fresh basil.

Add olive oil, dijon mustard, wine vinegar, fresh black pepper, salt, garlic, and oregano.

Cucumbers in Sour Cream

Peel cucumbers and onion, slice into rings.

Add sea salt and a little fresh chopped dill weed and Worcestershire.

Add just enough sour cream or plain unsweetened yogurt to bind.

Let stand for at least 3 hours.

Marinated Cucumbers

Peel cucumbers, seed with an apple corer, and slice into rings.

Dice medium red onions and red, green, and yellow bell peppers.

Marinate in a little of your favorite Italian dressings or try mine.

Marinated Asparagus

Peel the bottoms of fresh asparagus and steam or poach until al dente.

Shock in ice water to stop cooking and chill.

Top with Italian dressing and let marinate for at least 1 hour.

Waldorf Salad

Dice medium peeled celery root and freshly cored peeled apples.

Blend with walnuts and some orange zest.

Bind with 1 part sour cream and 1 part sweet whip cream to 3 parts mayonnaise, season with a little salt and fresh ground black pepper.

Marinated Fresh Fruit Salad

Dice medium honeydew, cantaloupe melon, fresh pineapple, apples.

Add just enough water to barely cover the fruit.

Add enough sugar and lemon and Chablis to barely taste it.

Marinate for at least 24 hours.

Italian Dressing

In the food processor place chunks of red onion, green bell pepper, celery, carrots, garlic, black and green olives. Add 3 ounces dijon mustard, 1 Tblsp dry basil, a little thyme, and even less oregano. Add an egg (whole, white, or just the yolk) and blend all, then slowly drizzle cottonseed or soybean oil into the mix while blending.

When thick, add wine vinegar, more oil, and more vinegar to taste and for desired consistency.

Add a little olive juice, taste, and add sea salt and fresh ground black pepper.

Specialty Cold Soup Recipes

Vichyssoise – Cold Potato Leek Soup

Remove all peel and eyes from chefs' potatoes and put in a pot.

Add a mild chicken stock to barely cover the potatoes.

Put a split washed leek on top and semi-cover the pot.

Simmer until the stock has been reduced to 1 cup.

Take out leek and refrigerate until well chilled.

Rice or smash potatoes and the leek, do not whip with a machine.

Hand whip into the potatoes, heavy cream, half & half, or milk to a soup consistency.

Add table salt, fresh ground black pepper.

Serve with a dollop of unsweetened whip cream and fresh chopped chives.

Gazpachio – Spanish-style Vegetable Soup

Pulse chunks of vegetables in food processor until fine chopped, equal amounts of celery, red onion, green bell peppers, and a little smashed garlic.

Add enough V8 juice to cover the vegetables, season with dried basil and thyme leaves and a little fresh cilantro.

Add a good amount of Worcestershire and fresh ground black pepper, a little tabasco, and sea salt, and pulse the mix to blend all.

Marinate for 24 hours, serve with a dollop of sour cream, chopped seeded cucumbers, and chopped cilantro.

Cantaloupe Bisque

Peel, seed, and cut chunks of ripe cantaloupe and put in food processor.

Puree until smooth and add just enough buttermilk to cream.

Add a little sweet white wine and sugar to taste.

Spiced

Make a thin paste by mixing cinnamon, allspice, a little clove, and water.

Simmer briefly and let cool.

Add a little at a time to the soup until desired flavor is reached.

Honeydew, Kiwi, and Grape Soup

Peel, seed, and cut chunks of ripe honeydew and put in food processor.

Add ripe peeled and cut kiwi and green grapes, puree all.

Add melon liqueur, sugar, and fresh lime juice to enhance flavor if needed.

Banana, Papaya, and Mango Soup

Peel, seed, and cut chunks of ripe papaya, mango, and banana.

Puree all and add lemon and orange zest to garnish and a little contreau or fruit liqueur for flavor.

Add orange juice until proper consistency is achieved.

Served with a dollop of sour cream that has been heated to just under a simmer.

Covered hot, blend in a little fruit liqueur if desired, and chilled for a day, which is termed crème fresh.

Strawberry Bisque

Cut 1 pint of very ripe strawberries and puree in a food processor until smooth.

Add just enough heavy cream to thicken and sugar if needed and lemon juice to taste.

Serve with a dollop of sweetened whip cream and a sprig of mint.

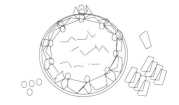

Vegetable Peel Designs

Spell out your occasion on a salad or the rim of a plate. Display is comprised of cucumber slices, radish slices, black olive slices, and red grape slices.

Specialty Slicing, Diamonds, and Strips

Uses: Decorate the Top of Salads, Dips, Plate Rims, Any Flat Surface
Tools: Sharp paring or French knife and a good potato peeler

Borders and garnishes are easy with vegetables. Display is comprised of cucumber slices, radish slices, cherry tomato, and black olives.

Tricks of the Trade

Diamonds, thin strips, and figures can be cut from the skin of any vegetable. Use a razor knife like a pen or a sharp tipped paring knife to cut out figures and separate the components of the figure. To make this black bird, first cut out the body, then the two wings. The separate components of a figure can be comprised of different vegetable skins and colors. From the basic designs illustrated here, many elaborate variations can be easily created.

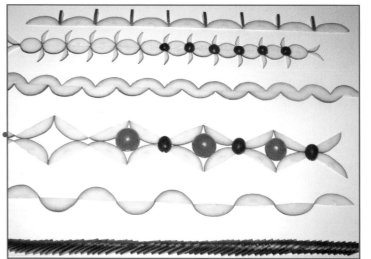

1. Square off the sides of the peel.

Display is comprised of the skin from eggplant, orange, carrot, cucumber, and radish.

2. Angle the knife to cut diamonds.

Specialty Slicing

Uses: Decorate the Top of Salads, Dips, Plate Rims, Any Flat Surface
Tools: Sharp paring or French knife and a good potato peeler

Cut the cucumber horizontally along the length.

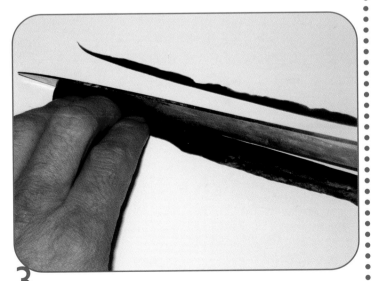

3. Cut a thin strip from the side of the peel.

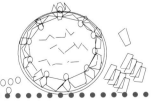

2. The thickness of this cut determines the thickness of the slices.

4. Radish, carrot, radish, black olive, and orange.

3. The bias angle cut will determine the length of the slices.

Tricks of the Trade

This style of garnishing is probably the most fun. Mother Nature did most of the work by creating all those colors produce has to offer. Now it is up to you to cut the produce into consistent shapes to "produce" your own masterpiece. This is only one basic cut that can create an infinite number of designs.

Salad and Table Centerpieces

Edible Centerpieces

Uses: Plate Garnishing, Salad Garnishing, and Food Holders
Tools: Sharp paring or French knife, channel knife, and a good potato peeler

Tricks of the Trade

These are great for Crudités trays and can be used to hold individual portions of food.

Thick Half Slices

Always use the other hand to guide the thickness of the cut. Keep the blade pointed down with the handle up, this will keep slices together. Cut the slices into even thicknesses for the best presentation.

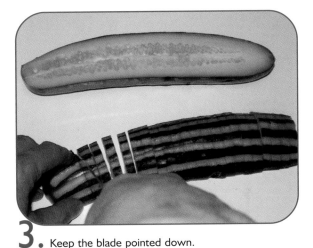

3. Keep the blade pointed down.

1. Cut cucumber through the middle length.

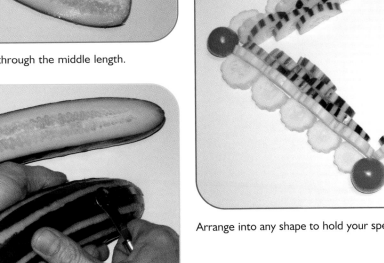

2. Channel out strips.

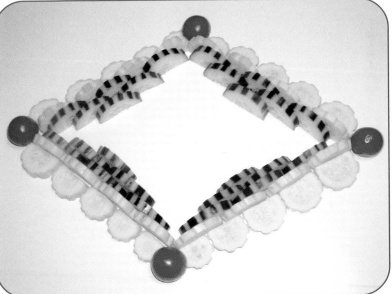

Arrange into any shape to hold your special treat!

Citrus Crowns

Uses: Plate Garnishing, Salad and Platter Garnishing, Centerpiece Displays
Tools: Sharp paring knife

Lemon crowns are common for lobster dishes, usually taking the cook some time to complete. That's why Lemon crowns are reserved for lobster or other upscale dishes. After you master this systematic method, you will find how easily and quickly you can create fantastic works of art that are sure to astound everyone. The crown cut technique is basically the same in all products.

Learn this skill and you are well on your way to creating many different edible masterpieces.

Tricks of the Trade

Table height is very important to properly handling knives. There should be just a slight bend in the arms when your hands are on the work surface. It is safer and easier to cut with a very sharp knife. From the basic designs illustrated here, many elaborate variations can be easily created.

Method

1. Find the perfect orange and cut off each end to make two flat bases.
2. Hold the orange between thumb and forefingers in left hand on a table directly in front of you. See how you can roll it on the table while holding onto it? This is key!
3. Hold the paring knife like a saw and position the blade at an angle to cut an upside down V, **see fig. 1**. Look straight down at the fruit and insert the blade a half inch from the top and about two-thirds into the fruit; with a sawing action cut down at the proper angle and stop about a half inch from the bottom of the orange, **see fig. 3**. Note: It is better to insert the blade two-thirds into the center of the fruit or vegetable.
4. The next cut starts at the same place as the last cut, only angle the blade in the opposite direction, **see fig. 2**. Repeat the process, this time positioning the blade in the opposite angle to complete the V.
5. After making a V, turn the fruit, not the knife, and proceed around until you meet the first V, **see fig. 4**.
6. Pull the orange apart; you have just carved two crowns, **see fig. 5**.

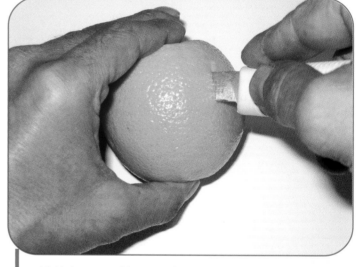

I. Hold the top and bottom of the orange and roll to reposition.

2. Angle the blade to cut a V. Use the knife like a saw for better control.

3. Be careful not to cut through the bottom.

5. Pull the crowns apart.

4. Turn the fruit, not the knife.

Practice makes it easy.

Squash and Cucumber Crowns and Flowers

Uses: Plate and Platter Garnishing, Salad Garnishing, and Hot Vegetable
Tools: Sharp paring knife

Tricks of the Trade

It is very important to pick fruits and vegetables that are of good color. There should not be any blemishes, and they should be uniformly shaped and sized.

Method

1. Pick out a nice fat cucumber or zucchini.
2. Cut both ends off to sit flat and then into 3-inch logs.
3. Hold the log between thumb and forefingers in left hand on a table. The product should be positioned so the length is facing you. See how you can roll it on the table while holding onto it (**see fig. 1**)? This is key.
4. Hold the paring knife like a saw and position the blade at an angle to cut an upside down V, **see fig. 2**. Look straight down at the log and insert the blade a half inch from the top and about two-thirds into the fruit. With a sawing action, cut down on the log at the proper angle. Stop about a half inch from the bottom of the log, **see fig. 3**. Note: It is better to insert the blade a little deeper than half way through the center.
5. The next cut is one half inch to the right of the first cut. Repeat the process, this time positioning the blade in the opposite angle to complete the V.
6. After making a V, turn the log, not the knife, and proceed until you meet the first V.
7. Pull the log apart.

To Turn Crown into Flowers

1. Stand crown on end and cut between rind and meat to a half inch from the base of the V, **see fig. 4**.
2. Dice six or seven quarter inch squares from the top or bottom of the cucumber that was cut earlier.
3. Insert a square, rind side down, between the rind and meat of the cucumber crown, **see fig. 5**.
4. To revive the tulips for a second or third use, soak in cold water.

1. Cut V's while turning the product, not the knife.

2. Start and stop a half inch from the ends.

3. Sawing V's with the knife.

5. Put a spacer in rind side down to open the petals.

4. Cut between the rind and meat.

Italian Roasted Squash Crowns

Preheat oven to 350 degrees.
1. Blend in a bowl olive oil, basil, garlic, salt, and pepper.
2. Lightly brush on squash crowns.
3. Stand crowns up on cooking sheet, top with Parmesan cheese.
4. Roast about fifteen minutes or until just tender.

Onion Crowns

Uses: Salad Garnishing, Platter Garnishing, Centerpieces, and Food Holders
Tools: Sharp paring knife

Tricks of the Trade

When purchasing, look for onions that are a single large bulb, without growths or bruises. You can use red, white or yellow onions; Vidalia is preferred if eating. A ripe onion is best. To alleviate strong odor and flavor, try soaking the onion cups in a mild vinegar solution.

Method

1. Pick out onions that have an even growth, with no soft spots. Be careful not to damage good skin.
2. Cut at least a half inch off the bottom, but less on top to make two flat bases.
3. Grasp the onion firmly between thumb and forefingers on a table. See how you can roll it on the table while holding onto it. This is key!
4. Hold the paring knife like a saw and position the blade at an angle to cut an upside down V, **see fig. 1**. Look straight down at the onion and insert the blade an inch from the top and about two thirds into the onion, with a sawing action cut down at the proper angle, stopping about one inch from the bottom of the onion. Note: It is better to insert the blade a little deeper than half way through the center.
5. The next cut is at the same place as the first, except position the blade in the opposite angle. Repeat the process this time positioning the blade in the opposite angle to complete the V.
6. After making a V, turn the fruit, not the knife, and proceed until you meet the first V.
7. Pull the onion apart; you have just carved two crowns.

• Use a secure grip, with the product on a table, to cut V's.

To Make Onion Crowns into Cups to Hold Food

Yield: 6 to 10 onion cups
Uses: Fill with Salads, Olives or Any Product That Goes With Onion

Method

1. Run warm water over the top of the crown while fanning ribs with fingers, **see fig. 2**.
2. Turn the onion over, grasping it with both hands on both sides.
3. Run under warm water and gently push with thumbs to loosen cups, **see fig. 3**.
4. Turn onion over and gently pull out cups.

2. Carefully fan out to loosen layers.

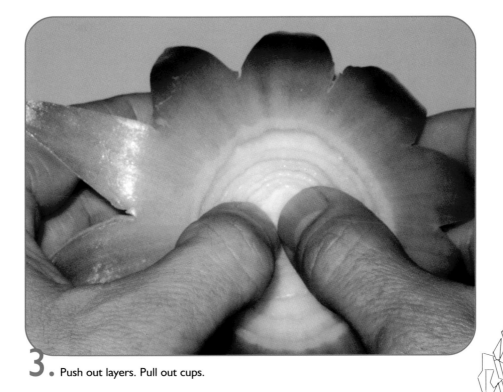

3. Push out layers. Pull out cups.

Onion Chrysanthemum

1. Peel an onion and trim off the top, do not trim the core end.
2. Place a peeled onion core side down in a jar that allows the onion to go in only an inch or so.
3. Cut down through the middle; the jar will stop the cut, **see fig. 1**.
4. Quarter turn the onion and make the cutting directly in the middle to form a cross.
5. Turn the onion again to make two more cuts directly in the middle, cutting directly through the middle of each wedge, cutting two at a time, leaving the onion still connected to the base, **see fig. 2**.
6. Open the wedges evenly to form an open flower, **see fig. 3**.
7. To add color, soak onion flower in a vinegar, water, and food coloring solution.

2. Turn the jar while center cutting.

1. Use a jar to stop from cutting too deep.

3. Gently fan the outer layers.

Vegetable Tulips

Uses: Plate and Platter Garnishing, Centerpiece Display, and Hot Vegetable
Tools: Sharp paring knife and a good potato peeler

Tricks of the Trade

To peel a carrot, hold the tip with one hand and with the other hand peel in long downward strokes. Spin the carrot, not the peeler, to assure a smooth, round surface. Tulips can be made days in advance or reused twice if held in cold water. After carrots are peeled, soak in hot water to soften and brighten color. Zucchini is an easy vegetable to carve tulips from.

Method

1. Pick out a straight, fat, good color cucumber.
2. Hold the cucumber by the base with one hand.
3. Position the paring knife in the other with your thumb on the bottom, **see fig. 1**.
4. Lay the blade against the side of the cucumber and angle the blade to about forty-five degrees.
5. Pull the blade into the cucumber a little over half way and remove the blade, **see fig. 2**.
6. Turn the cucumber, not the knife, and repeat the step two more times, **see fig. 3**.
7. Detach crowns; now you have a guideline to go by, **see fig. 4**.

Notice that the tulips get larger with every cut; use this fact for decorating purposes. Cucumber sliced on the bias can be easily cut progressively larger. Put standing tulips on a fanned display of bias cut cucumber or in the center of a hicama daisy. To stand tulips up, position a tulip on its side to cut the bottom flat.

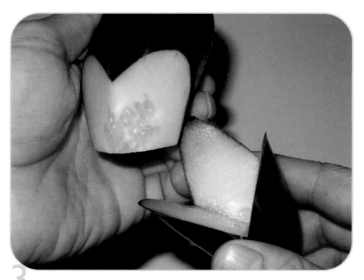

3. Stuck? Twist off or cut the tulip at a deeper angle.

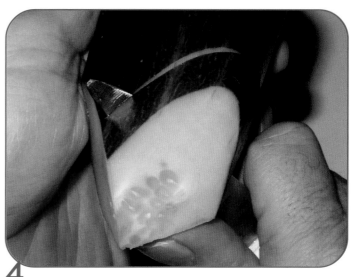

4. Now its easier, the first cuts left guidelines. More angle means longer petals.

1. Use your thumb to pull the blade down.

2. Turn the product one-third turn after each petal cut.

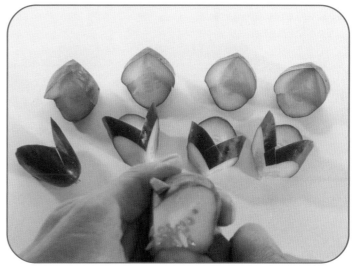

Note the gradual change in size; use this fact in your garnishing scheme.

Specialty Tulip Recipes

Tricks of the Trade

For sautéing purposes, first drop vegetables in boiling water until just tender, shock in cool water, and drain.

Spices and herbs are sautéed briefly before adding vegetables to draw out oils and to coat vegetables.

Briefly toss vegetables in the seasoned hot oil until vegetables are hot.

Italian Style: Sauté tulips in olive oil with basil, thyme, garlic, salt, black pepper, and chablis.

Swiss Style: Sauté in cottonseed oil with anise seed, a drop of Worcestershire, salt, and pepper.

Oriental style: Sauté in peanut oil with ginger, garlic, soy sauce, water chestnuts, and sake.

My Favorite: Sauté butter with dill and sea salt, lightly toss carrot tulips until hot.

Tulip Salad: Blend your favorite tulips with cottonseed oil and white vinegar to taste, marinate for 24 hours, taste, and add seasoning if needed.

Tomato Rose

Uses: Plate Garnishing, Platter Garnishing, and Centerpiece Display.
Tools: Sharp paring or French knife

Tricks of the Trade

Look for fruits and vegetables that are firm and with good, rich colors. There are many types of tomatoes, oranges, and grapefruit. Don't worry about making the rose strip paper-thin; the tomato rose looks better when the skin is cut a little thick. Roses can also be made a day in advance.

Method
1. Hold a tomato upside down in one hand.
2. Using the knife like a saw, carefully begin to take a slice off the bottom, **see fig. 1**. Just before cutting completely through, turn the knife, **see fig. 2**.
3. Begin to take off about a one-inch wide strip of skin.
4. Continue using your knife like a saw while turning the tomato—turn the tomato, not the knife! **see fig. 3, 4.**
5. Position the skin to its natural form; the slice you first cut is the base, **see fig. 5 and 6**.

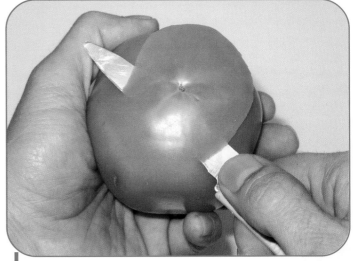

1. This is the base for the rose.

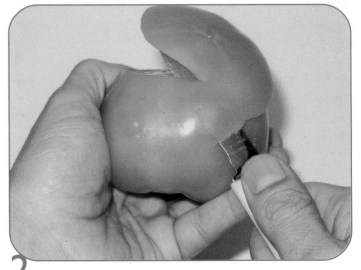

2. Begin to cut a strip off the entire tomato.

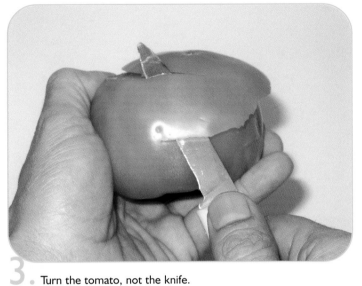

3. Turn the tomato, not the knife.

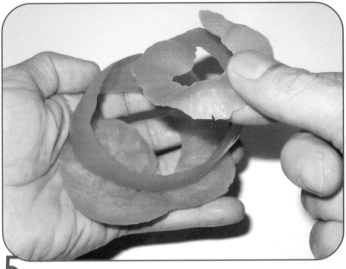

5. Let the skin go to its natural curve.

4. Cut all of the skin off.

6. Twist to compact the rose.

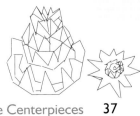

Tomato Star

Uses: Salad Holder and Centerpiece Garnish
Tools: Sharp paring or French knife

Method

1. Wash and core the tomato.
2. Place the tomato, core side down, on cutting surface.
3. Cut down through the middle, stopping about one inch short of cutting the tomato in half.
4. Turn the tomato and make the same cut to form a cross.
5. Turn the tomato again to make two more cuts to form eight sections still connected at the base.
6. Open the wedges evenly to form an open flower.

Note: Salad can be served on this creative base. Position slices of fresh mozzarella on the side of the wedges. Season with a little olive oil, sea salt, and fresh ground black pepper on the tomato before placing the salad. A large ice cream scoop is a good way to place any mayonnaise-based salad on neatly. Just be sure to leave the edge showing so everyone can see a well-trimmed and colorful display.

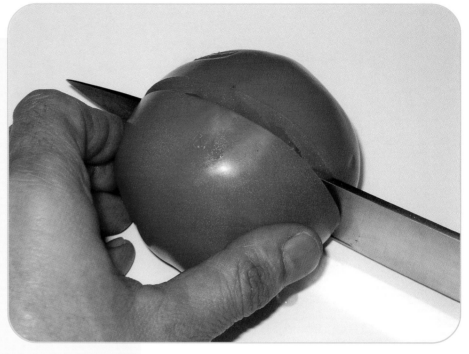

See the glass method in the Onion Chrysanthemum section.

Core the tomato and turn it upside down.

Don't cut through. Four cuts total.

Potato and Apple Mushrooms

Uses: Plate Garnishing, Platter Garnishing, and Centerpiece Display
Tools: Sharp paring or French knife and an apple corer

Tricks of the Trade

To keep a potato or apple white, soak it in a lemon water solution. The stronger the lemon solution is and the longer you marinate, the whiter it will keep. Mushrooms can be made a day ahead if stored in cool water with a little lemon. From the basic designs illustrated here, many elaborate variations can be easily created.

Method

1. Dip the corer into water so it slides easily through the apple or potato.
2. Insert the corer two-thirds into the end of the apple or potato, about an inch from the top, **see fig. 1**.
3. With the corer still in the apple or potato, lay it down on its side, width facing you.
4. Cut an inch from the top of the apple or potato, hitting the knife blade against the coring tool, **see fig. 2**.
5. Roll the apple or potato straight—do not move the knife—until the knife meets the first cut.
6. Pull the apple or potato off and soak in cold water, or lemon water if it is not intended to be cooked.
7. Rings are used to hold up the mushroom by inserting the stem of mushroom in the hole, **see fig. 3**.

2. The core tool stops the knife from cutting through. Spin the product, not the knife.

1. Insert a core tool two-thirds deep through the bottom core of the apple.

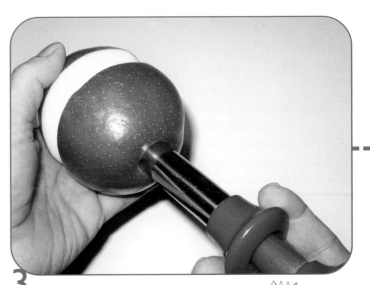

3. Use the plunger to push the mushroom stem out of the core tool.

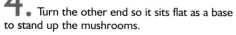

4. Turn the other end so it sits flat as a base to stand up the mushrooms.

5. Cut strips with a channel knife.

This can be fried, roasted with olive oil, rosemary, and garlic, or boiled in chicken stock, butter, and parsley.

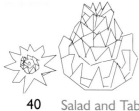

Potato Daisy Arrangements

Uses: Plate Garnishing, Platter Garnishing, and Centerpiece Display
Tools: Sharp paring or French knife and a two inch daisy cookie cutter

Tricks of the Trade

Cut potatoes should be soaked in lemon water if they are to be used as a garnish or plain water a day or two in advance if intended to be cooked. The length of time you soak the potato determines how long it will stay white, ten minutes is okay for same day usage. For this centerpiece, daisies and the base can be cut out of any solid fruit or vegetable; for flowers I prefer diacon root or potato. The two-inch daisy cutter may be found in any cooking store.

Ingredients

Large baking potatoes, red grapes, lemon juice, scallions, and wood skewers.

Method

1. Slice potato in quarter inch slices and put directly into water.
2. Use a cookie cutter to cut out daisies and soak in lemon water for at least 5 minutes, **see fig. 1**.
3. Cut the tops off red or black grapes or the bottoms off black olives or slices of green olives.
4. Cut the bulbs off scallions and reserve green stalks, **see fig. 2**.
5. Cut the bottom off an eggplant or an evenly shaped potato to make a base to hold the flowers.
6. Stick the flat end of a skewer in the center of the base and follow around that skewer with five more. Surround those five with twelve more skewers to create a large symmetrical arrangement.
7. Put a scallion stalk over the skewer to cover; if it is too long, pull 1 side down to resemble a leaf.
8. Place daisy on each skewer top and push down until it pokes out of the top of the flower, **see fig. 3**.
9. Place a grape top in the center of the daisy. Voila! **See fig. 4 and 5**.

Tip:

You don't have to make a large bouquet, in two minutes a single flower can be created. Use a real glass vase made to hold one flower and your guests will think it is real.

1. Cut daisies and soak in lemon.

2. Cut scallion tops for stems; insert a wood skewer.

3. Position the skewers point end up.

4. Push the daisy down to expose a point.

5. Place a grape top on the point to secure.

Carrot and Diacon Radish Production Flowers

Hold the tip to peel carrot's length with a downward stroke, turning to peel evenly round. With a channel knife cut a series of grooves through the length that are evenly spaced. Cut slices about 1/8" thick. Use in the same way as the potato daisies and make a salad or a hot vegetable dish.

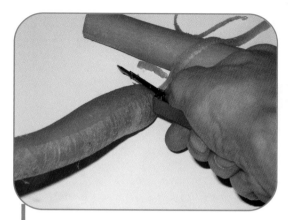

1. Peel a carrot round and smooth.

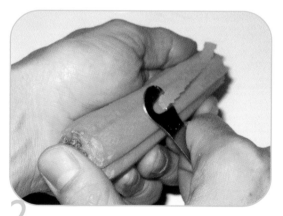

2. Channel out strips.

3. Slice and create ...

Fruit Fantasia

Melon Crowns

Uses: Platter Garnishing, Centerpieces, and Food Holders.
Tools: Sharp paring knife and a sharp French knife

Tricks of the Trade

All fruits and vegetables should be thoroughly washed before cutting. Any melon can be utilized; I prefer an extra large honeydew or casaba melon. Any meaty fruit or vegetable will expand, opening flowers more, if soaked in cold water. This is the same procedure as outlined in the Orange, Squash, and Onion Crown directions. From the basic designs illustrated here, many elaborate variations can be easily created.

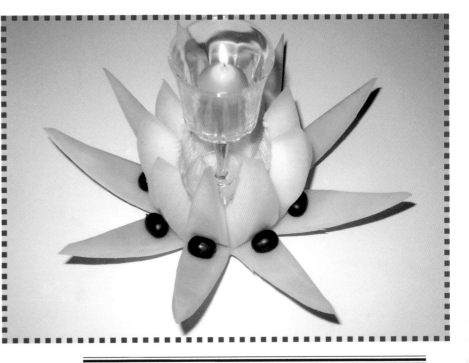

Method

1. Find an even shaped honeydew melon with a uniform color.
2. Cut a little off each end to make two flat bases.
3. Put your left hand on top of the melon on a table directly in front of you.
4. Now, holding a paring knife like a saw and positioning the blade at an angle to cut a V, look straight down at the fruit and insert the blade about one inch from the top. With a sawing action, cut down at the proper angle to make the first cut of the V. Stop cutting about one inch from the bottom.
5. Insert the blade again at the top of the melon, about 2 inches from the first cut. This time angle the blade in the opposite direction to meet the bottom of the V, **see fig. 1.**
6. After making a V, turn the melon, not the knife, and proceed to meet the first V cut made, **see fig. 2.**
7. Pull the melon apart and gently scoop out the seeds with your hand, **see fig. 3.**
8. Wash out any remaining seeds under cold water.

To make this crown resemble a flower:

1. Stand the crown on end and cut between the rind and meat to a half inch from the base of the V, **see fig. 4.**
2. Dice seven or eight half inch squares from the top or bottom of the melon that was cut earlier.
3. Insert a grape or a piece of rind between the rind and meat of the melon crown to open rind, **see fig. 5.**
4. To revive for a second use, soak in warm water, or third use, soak in cold lemon water.
5. Enhance with a votive candle in a champagne glass inserted into the melon.

• Cut an upside down V.

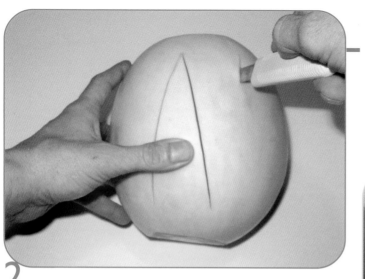

2. Turn the melon, not the knife.

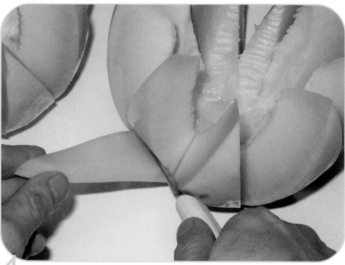

4. Cut between rind and meat.

3. Pull apart and remove seeds.

5. Place grapes between the rind and the meat.

Bird Cage

Uses: Platter Garnishing, Centerpieces, and Food Holders
Tools: Sharp paring knife and French knife, 12 inch wood skewers

Tricks of the Trade

Adjust the position of the product so cuts are easily accessible. Always turn the product, not the knife, when doing repetitious cutting. All garnishes are interchangeable with other fruits and vegetables. Pick out firm produce so centerpiece can be used three times or more. Soak in tepid water the first time to revive and cold water after that.

Method

1. Position the melon on its side to cut a slice off the bottom in one knife stroke to create a flat base. Stand the melon up. If it does not stand straight, take another complete slice off the bottom; if the melon leans to the left, take more of a slice off the right side to level.
2. Draw a guideline line around the melon one inch from the top.
3. Insert the blade at an angle and pull the blade straight out, **see fig. 1**.
4. Insert the blade in opposite angle to form a V cut and repeat the process.
5. Take the top off the melon, deseed and rinse out seeds, and chalk in cold water.
6. Using a channel knife, or with the tip of a sharp paring knife, cut between Vs to remove strips off the top and the base, **see fig. 2**.
7. Push 3 skewers through the melon to touch the table, position with the point end up, **see fig. 3**.
8. Insert red or black grapes end to end to cover the skewers, **see fig. 4**.
9. Put the top on skewers while holding them slightly together and positioning, **see fig. 5**.
10. Decorate with two plum love birds kissing, bride and groom figurines, or hollow out the base with a spoon and fill with your favorite fruit salad.

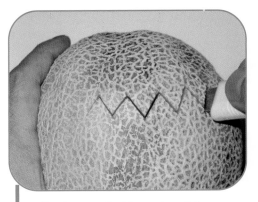

1. Cut the top off with a series of V cuts. Turn the melon.

2. Carve V strips with the tip of a sharp knife.

3. Break skewers to desired height and position point end up.

4. Place whole grapes end to end on the skewer to cover the wood.

5. Position the top and decorate with plum birds, see Apple Love Birds.

Wedding Carriage

Uses: Platter Garnishing, Centerpiece
Tools: Sharp paring knife and French knife, square wood toothpicks

Tricks of the Trade

Use square wooden toothpicks to connect one piece of produce to another. Look for produce that is firm, with a good color and shaped evenly. Pick out firm produce so centerpiece can be used three times or more. Soak in tepid water the first time to revive and cold water after that.

Method

1. Pick out one large, oblong-shaped honeydew with no blemishes (unless it's on the bottom side) and two small, oblong-shaped, average-sized, firm cantaloupes.
2. Slice off a small slice from the bottom of the honeydew so it sits flat.
3. Using the tip of the knife, insert the blade in the top and jig like a saw to cut out a lid, **see fig. 1**. Remove the top, deseed, and rinse out inside of the melon and top.
4. Score the lid and sides of the melon with a channel knife, **see fig. 2**, or use the tip of a sharp paring knife to cut V wedge lines.
5. Trim thick wood skewers to desired height and position correctly to hold the roof in position. Place whole grapes end to end to cover the wood skewers, but leave the tips exposed, **see fig. 3**, and attach the lid.
6. Cut four center slices, 1" thick from the width of the cantaloupe. Note how the two center slices match and the two outer slices match. Use one set in the front and one in the back. Using an open soup or vegetable can that is the proper size, cut a ring out of the center to form wheels, **see fig. 4**.
7. Cut four equal half inch thick center slices of lemon or lime (I used leftover apple ends) for wheel hubs.
8. Push five toothpicks into each of the four cantaloupe wheels half way, **see fig. 5**.
9. Place a wheel on the table flat and position the lemon slice, then push the wood picks all the way in to secure the lemon slice into position. Use something hard and flat to push the wood picks out of sight, but not the knife. Then trim the bottom slightly so the wheel has a flat surface to stand on.
10. Position a wheel and mark the side of the melon where the wheel rind meets the carriage. Push a wood pick into that point, leaving it half exposed. Then attach the wheels by pushing them into place.
11. For the fenders, cut two thick center slices from an orange and cut those in half. Push a pick into each wheel, and then attach the half slices of orange.
12. Fill with flowers, fruit salad, or parsley and decorate with a bride and groom figurine.

1. Cut out roof of carriage.

2. Use the channel knife as shown.

3. Tips of skewers are exposed.

4. Use a soup can as a cutter.

5. Push the wood picks in half way, position the center, then push the picks all the way in.

6. Put a one inch piece of wood pick in the center of the wheel with the tip exposed to secure a grape.

Baby Carriage

Uses: *Platter Garnishing, Centerpieces, Salad Holder*
Tools: *Sharp paring knife and French knife, square wood toothpicks*

Tricks of the Trade

Use square wooden toothpicks to connect one piece of produce to another. Look for produce that is firm, with a good color, and shaped evenly. Pick out firm produce so the centerpiece can be used up to three times—soak it in tepid water the first time to revive and cold water after that.

Method

1. Pick out one large, oblong-shaped honeydew with no blemishes, unless they are on the bottom side.
2. Pick out one firm cantaloupe; the length of the cantaloupe should be the same size as the width of the honeydew.
3. Cut the honeydew in half through the navel and deseed.
4. Cut off a small slice from the bottom of the honeydew side to sit flat.
5. Cut the cantaloupe in half, then cut one half in the center length to make a wedge.
6. Match up the cut melon to assure a good fit, **see fig. 1**.
7. Trim the meat off the cantaloupe as shown, **see fig. 2**.
8. Cut V strips to simulate a carriage bonnet's folds, **see fig. 3**.
9. With a spoon, scoop out some meat from the honeydew if desired.
10. Cut a one inch wide strip from the center of the half of the cantaloupe for the carriage handle.
11. Cut away excess meat from the handle using the same method as seen in **figure 2**.
12. Attach the handle with picks and position, **see fig. 4**.
13. Cut two half inch thick center slices from two oranges.
14. Position an orange slice and push a wood pick into the melon where it meets the orange rind, **see fig. 5**.
15. Attach the back of the orange wheel rind to the exposed wood pick.
16. Fill with your favorite fruit salad or dip and position bonnet securely with picks.

1. Trim the bottom to sit flat.

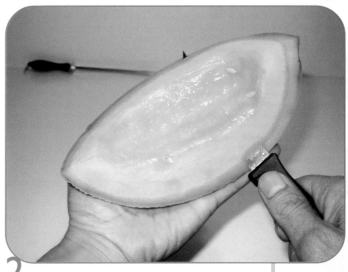

2. Trim excess meat off the bonnet.

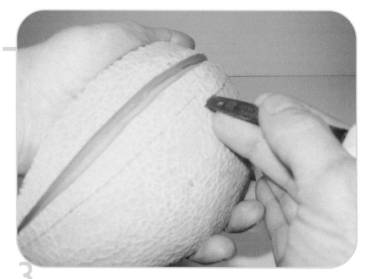

3. Cut V strips to simulate folds.

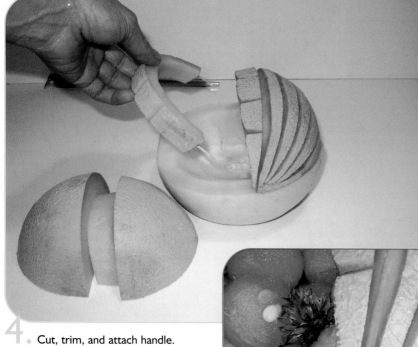

4. Cut, trim, and attach handle.

5. Attach rind of orange to the pick.

Mute Swan and Peacock

Uses: *Platter Garnishing, Centerpieces, and Food & Candle Holders*
Tools: *Sharp vegetable knife*

Tricks of the Trade

Those pumpkin carving books work on melons too, using the same principal.

Method

1. Draw a pattern onto the melon with an erasable marker, **see fig. 1**.
2. With a vegetable knife, insert the entire blade in the tip of the right wing. Utilizing a jigsaw action continue until you get past the top of the beak and withdraw the blade.
3. Insert the blade pointed in the opposite direction to cut the underside of the beak, **see fig. 2**.
4. Continue: when you get to the neck, jig knife in a very short saw action and turn the blade at the same time, continue to form the wing, meeting the previous wing tip, **see fig. 3**.
5. To carve the back side of the wings, turn the melon so the side is facing you. Start the cut at the back top center and cut down the backside of a wing, then circle up to cut the tail, aiming toward a center angle and ending the cut at the tip of the tail, **see fig. 5**.
6. Repeat the processes on the other side.
7. Carefully remove all pieces; insert a knife at an angle to pull the piece out, **see fig. 4**. Cut between the rind and the meat behind the head, neck, tail, and wings, **see fig. 6**.
8. Carve out the wing feathers with a channel knife or carve them with a paring knife, **see fig. 7**.
9. Insert the knife a half inch deep, using the thumb for leverage; angle the blade to cut a V. Repeat the first cut, angling the blade in the opposite direction to meet the first cut to make a long, thin wedge, remove, and continue to the bottom of the wing, then do the other side.

2. Cut up to form the bottom of the beak.

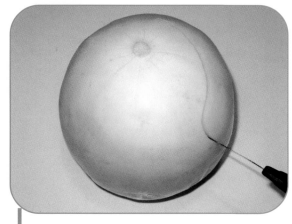

1. Trace the pattern with the knife tip.

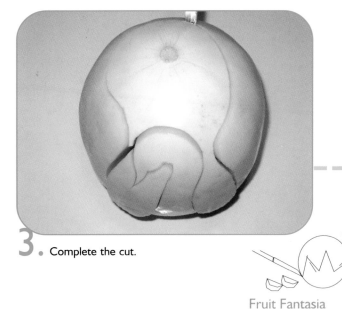

3. Complete the cut.

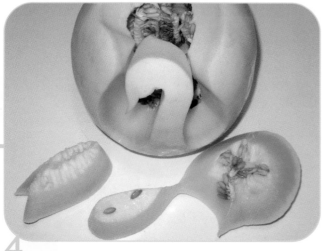

4. Remove sections.

7. Cut V strips with a paring knife or a channel knife.

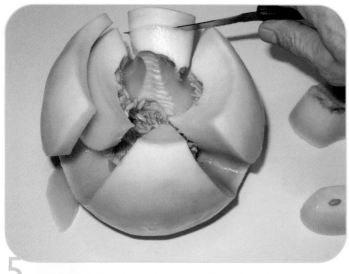

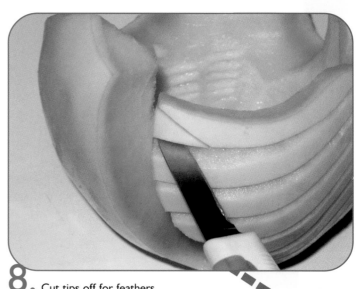

5. Cut behind the wing and turn up to form the tail.

8. Cut tips off for feathers.

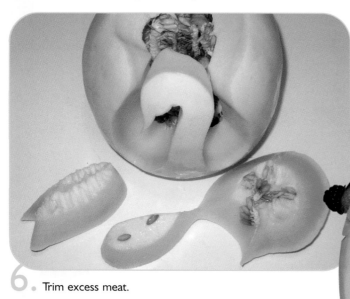

6. Trim excess meat.

This swan can be turned into a peacock by adding fruit skewers.

Watermelon Swan

Uses: Platter Garnishing, Centerpieces, and Food & Candle Holders
Tools: Sharp vegetable knife

Tricks of the Trade

Any pattern can be traced, cut out, and used over and over by soaking in tepid or cold water. This swan can be turned into a peacock by adding fruit skewers.

Method

Draw a pattern onto the melon with an erasable marker, **see fig. 1, 2, 3**.

1. With a vegetable knife, insert the entire blade in the tip of the right wing, **see fig. 5**. Utilizing a jigsaw action, continue until you get past the top of the beak and withdraw the blade.

2. Insert the blade pointed in the opposite direction to cut the underside of the beak, **see fig. 4**.

3. Continue: when you get to the neck jig the knife in a very short saw action and turn the blade at the same time, continuing to form the wing, meeting the previous wing tip, **see fig. 5**.

4. To carve the back sides of the wings, turn the melon so the side is facing you. Start the cut at the back top center and cut down the back side of a wing, then circle up to cut the tail, aiming toward a center angle and ending the cut at the tip of the tail.

5. Repeat processes on the other side.

6. Carefully remove all pieces, inserting a knife at an angle to pull the piece out, **see fig. 6**. Cut between the rind and the meat behind the head, neck, tail, and wings, **see fig. 7**.

7. Carve out the wing feathers with a channel knife or carve them with a paring knife, **see fig. 8, 9**. Insert the knife a half inch deep, using the thumb for leverage; angle the blade to cut a V. Repeat the first cut, angling the blade in the opposite direction to meet the first cut to make a long thin wedge, remove, and continue to the bottom of the wing, then the other side.

• Trace with an erasable marker.

2. Trace wings evenly on both sides.

3. Trace out the tail.

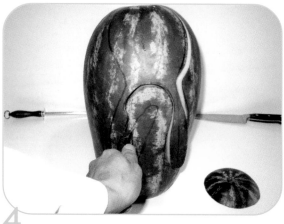

4. Start at the tip of right wing.

5. Make one continuous cut, ending at the tip of the left wing.

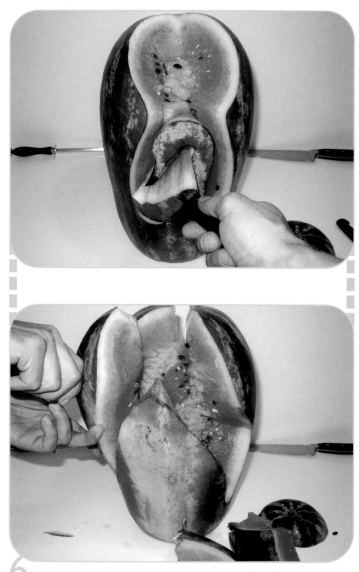

6. Pull out sections.

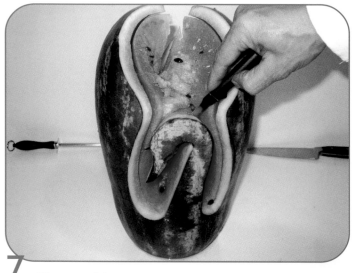

7. Trim around the carving to remove meat.

8. Cut V strips for the feathers.

9. Cut between the tips to separate.

Watermelon Wedding Vase

**Uses: Platter Garnishing, Centerpieces, and Food &
Candle Holders**
Tools: Sharp vegetable knife

Tricks of the Trade

Any pattern can be traced and cut out. Use sticker numbers and letters to personalize this carving. Pick out firm produce so the centerpiece can be used many times. Soak in tepid water before second use to revive and cold lemon water after third and even a fourth use.

Method

1. Trace a half pattern onto a folded sheet of paper, open the paper for an even-sided sketch, or get a made pattern from a stencil and coloring books.
2. Cut the pattern out with scissors.
3. Cut the bottom of the melon to sit evenly.
4. Holding the paper by the edge, dip into water, then position onto the melon, **see fig. 1**.
5. Starting from the top while utilizing the vegetable knife like a saw, insert the blade fully, and begin to saw out the pattern, **see fig. 2**.

I. Position the template.

6. Insert the tip of the blade at an angle in the section that needs to be removed and pull, **see fig. 3, 4**.
7. To hollow out, insert the blade fully about a half inch from the rind and saw around all edges, **see fig. 5**.
8. Use a spoon to scoop out the remaining meat, and rinse in cold water.
9. Cut V wedge strips to outline the heart and to decorate the bird's wings, **see fig. 6**.
10. Enhance the effect with a candle inside the carving. Dim the lights.
11. Fill with your favorite fresh berries.
12. Perfect for a large flower arrangement.

2. Always begin at the top.

3. Pull out all the unwanted pieces.

5. Continue to cut away the meat.

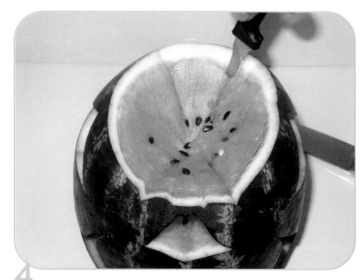

4. Cut away the meat from the rind.

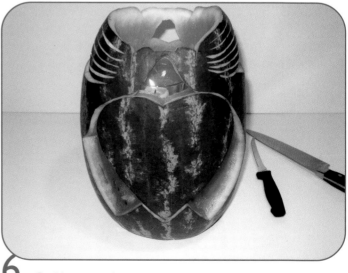

6. Cut V strips to decorate.

Pineapple Sailboat

Uses: *Platter Garnishing, Centerpieces, and Food Holders*
Tools: *Sharp French knife or a slicing knife, 10 inch wood skewers*

Tricks of the Trade

Buy a half pineapple and ask the deli to cut a thin slice on a slicing machine with the top facing the blade; this is the sail. Pick out a firm pineapple.

Method

1. Cut the pineapple stalk down by half.
2. With a sawing action cut the pineapple in half down the center, leaving the stalk on each side.
3. Carefully cut a quarter inch slice off the face with some leaves connected, **see fig. 1**.
4. Cut a slice from the bottom of the pineapple so it sits flat.
5. Push the skewer through the top of the pineapple slice, **see fig. 2**.
6. Push 5 red grapes end to end on the skewer, **see fig. 2**.
7. Push the tip of the skewer through the bottom of the pineapple slice to create the sails, **see fig. 3**.
8. Position the sail and push down on the skewer to secure and pull up the sail.
9. Place a grape on top to hide the skewer.

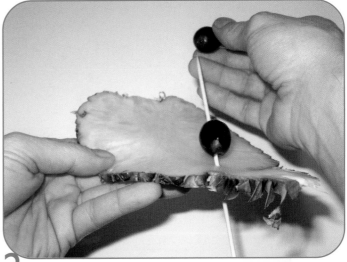

2. Use a thick wood skewer.

1. Cut a thin slice from a half pineapple.

3. Cover with grapes and attach.

Sectioned Fruit Wedge

Uses: *Platter Garnishing, Plate Centerpiece*
Tools: *Sharp French knife or a slicing knife, 10 inch wood skewers*

Method

1. Pick out a ripe pineapple and trim the stalk to half.
2. Lay the pineapple down, use your knife like a saw, start at the stalk end, and cut in half.
3. Cut again in the middle of the core to make 4 to 6 wedges.
4. Using a vegetable knife, position the blade to just under the core and saw completely around.
5. Do not cut the core. Slice half inch sections and push out sections alternately, **see bottom fig. 1, 2**.

1. • Use a vegetable knife like a saw.

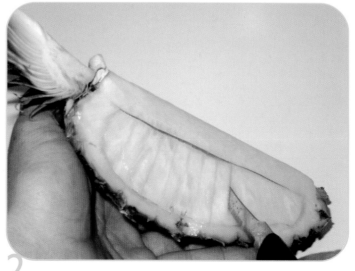

2. • Cut slices without cutting core.

Apple Love Birds

Uses: Platter Garnishing, Centerpieces, and Food Holders
Tools: Sharp French knife or paring knife

Tricks of the Trade

Soak apples in straight lemon juice to retain the white color. Check apples carefully for soft spots and shape. Use different colors and sizes.

Method

1. Stand apple on end; if it has a hump, center it on the opposite side.
2. Position the blade on the stem end in the center and angle it out a little to slice off a side.
3. Cut a half inch strip through the length of that slice, trim the meat to curve with the skin, **see fig. 1**. Cut a V shape at the end that curves the most for the beak.
4. Lay the apple flat side down and visualize 3 equal sections: the center for the tail and the remaining sections for the left and right wings.
5. Position the knife an eighth inch off the center on the length of the apple.
6. Saw the knife and gently push down to make the first cut of a V, **see fig. 2**.
7. Position the blade on the other side to cut a small wedge, which is the beginning of your tail.
8. Continue to cut three to five more wedges as thin as possible without breaking, **see fig. 3, 4**. As you cut wedges, put them directly into lemon juice, keeping the tail and each wing separate. When the second wing is complete, take the first set out of the lemon brine and assemble.
9. Replace all feathers and wings to their original position and fan out. Be careful not to mix up the wings, **see fig. 5**. Wings can be pushed back together, refrigerated, and fanned out before service, **see fig. 6**.

1. Side bias cut and cut middle strip.

2. Cut away meat for neck.

3. Start the center wing first.

5. Do not mix up the wedges.

4. Continue with right and left wings.

6. Push the wedges back together until ready for use.

Apple Fans

Uses: Platter Garnishing, Centerpieces, and Food Holders
Tools: Sharp French knife or paring knife

Method
1. Cut a thin bias slice off the end of a cucumber, squash, or your favorite fruit or vegetable.
2. Angle side slices to a point toward the tip's center.
3. Push down slightly to one side and fan out.

2. Push slightly to fan out.

1. Bias end cut or wedge.

3. Soak in lemon water.

Easter Bunny

1. Cut melons level.

2. Cut straight in.

Uses: Platter Garnishing, Centerpieces
Tools: French knife, sharp, vegetable knife, square wood toothpicks

Tricks of the Trade

Pick out melons with no blemishes, good color, and that are firm. Match up cantaloupes to the honeydew for proper proportion of head and body.

Ingredients

A large, firm, unblemished honeydew melon, 2 firm cantaloupes, 1 carrot, 1 black grape, and wood skewers

Method

1. Cut the bottom even to sit flat and cut the top even to hold the head of the rabbit level, **see fig. 1**.
2. Cut the bottom of the cantaloupe to match the top of the honeydew.
3. Insert the tip of the paring knife one half inch straight in the side and cut a ring for the upper leg, **see fig. 2**.
4. Lay the blade on the side of the first to cut a wedge around the upper leg, **see fig. 3**.
5. Carve the other side in the same shape, and then position the melons to get the best form, **see fig. 4**.
6. For the eyes, make a horizontal cut on the face of the cantaloupe a little less than half way down.
7. For the face, make a diagonal cut into the side to meet the first cut and remove the piece.
8. For the mouth, do the same cuts as the eyes, only upside down, **see fig. 8**.
9. For the teeth, square out a carrot slice and cut a V down the middle and position on face, **see fig. 12**.
10. Slice a peeled carrot on the bias one-eighth-inch thick and cut a black grape in half and arrange eyes.
11. For the ears, position two toothpicks where the ears should be and cut an eye-shaped hole there, **see fig. 9**.
12. Slice the meat off six cantaloupe wedges and insert a toothpick into the bottom of two of them, **see fig. 10**.
13. Place two wedges with picks into holes and position for ears; attach paws, **see fig. 13**.
14. Cut the other four wedge rinds square on one side and carve toes with a channel or paring knife.

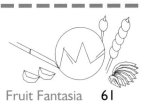

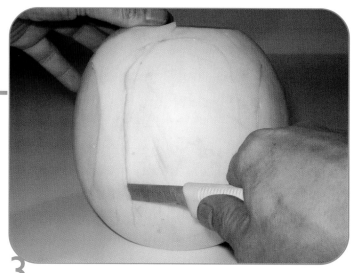

3. Cut at an angle.

4. Use this as a guide.

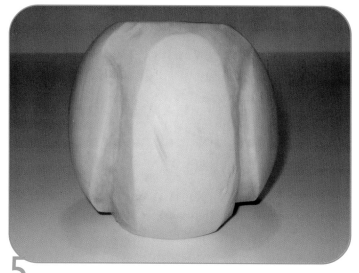

5. Cut hips evenly.

6. Two cuts for eyes.

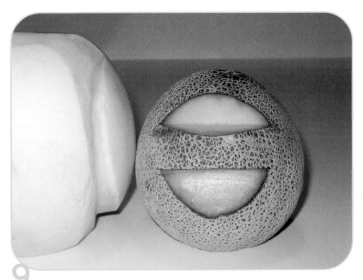

9. Use this as a guide.

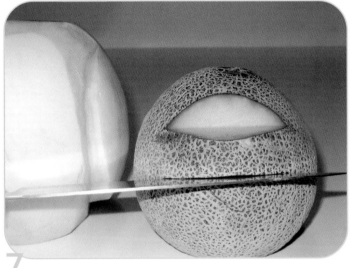

7. Two cuts for mouth.

10. Cut 4 wedges of cantaloupe.

8. The mouth is a deeper cut.

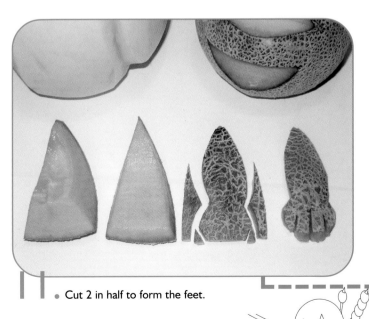

11. Cut 2 in half to form the feet.

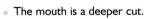

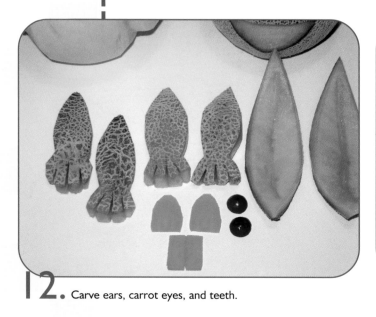

12. Carve ears, carrot eyes, and teeth.

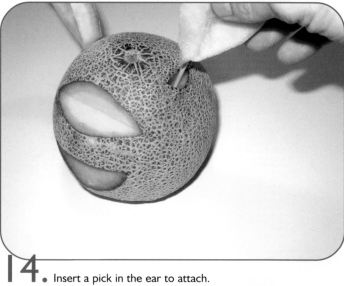

14. Insert a pick in the ear to attach.

13. Position ears and cut holes to insert.

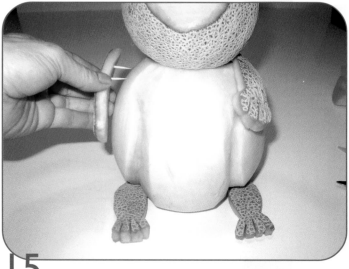

15. Attach arms and position legs.

Melon Basket

Uses: Platter Garnishing, Centerpieces, and Food Holders
Tools: Sharp paring knife and a sharp slicing knife

Method

1. Cut off the bottom or the side of the melon to sit flat.
2. Using the slicing knife like a saw, cut 1 inch off the center straight down, stopping half way, **see fig. 1**.
3. Make a horizontal cut to meet the vertical cut and remove the pieces.
4. Using the vegetable knife like a saw, cut where the meat turns to rind and form a handle, **see fig. 2**.
5. Score the inside of the melon into cubes but do not remove, **see fig. 3**.
6. Cut V shapes on the rim of the basket and tie a ribbon around the top of the handle, **see fig. 4**.
7. Put your favorite cut fruit arrangement on top of the flat base. Note: you can make this garnish from any round produce of any size.

1. Make a vertical cut off center, stopping half way, then cut horizontally to meet the first cut.

2. To create a guide for the other side, position the blade flat on the base. Keep it level and push through the melon. Cut a section from the other side to match the first.

3. Cut a continuous row of V's angling to the center.

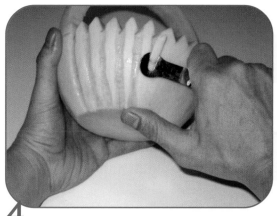

4. Channel knife sides to achieve a basket effect.

Melon Sculpture

Any type of melon can be utilized in this type of Rind Sculpture.

Sea Shells and Melon Daisy

Carving Melons

Uses: Platter Presentations, Personalized Centerpieces
Tools: French knife, vegetable knife, and paring knife

Tricks of the Trade

Use firm fruits and vegetables. Carvings can last up to a week. Soak carving pieces in water and lemon to revive.

Always work the knife like a jigsaw with short, quick jerks and light pressure for ultimate control.

Use square wooden picks to attach pieces or break long wood skewers and trim with wire cutters.

Use coloring book drawings as templates. Draw with the tip of the knife or poke holes to trace the figure. From the basic designs illustrated here, many elaborate variations can be easily created.

The meat of the melon is always displayed out. All colors of the rind and meat can be part of the display. To use a Parisian scoop, lay the flat side of the scoop against a flat side of the melon, push down, and twist.

Method

1. Position the melon on its side to face you horizontally.
2. Lay the blade vertically across the side of the melon and cut one third slice off the side.
3. Position a template and transfer an image or draw on the meat side with the tip of a knife.
4. Grasp the product in one hand on a table and use a vegetable or a paring knife like a saw, **see fig. 1**.
5. Trim off excess melon, **see fig. 2**.
6. Utilize the tip of the knife blade to cut long, straight V slices for decoration, **see fig. 3**.
7. Cut the tips round to resemble a shell.
8. Use sturdy wooden picks or skewers to connect, support, and suspend sculpture.
9. Place a strawberry in the center, surround with melon balls, and seal seams with grape quarters to create daisies.

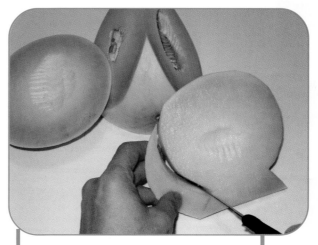

Trace and cut the shell form.

2. Level off excess meat.

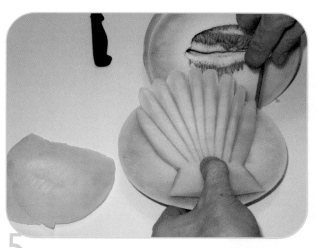

5. Trace the shell to duplicate.

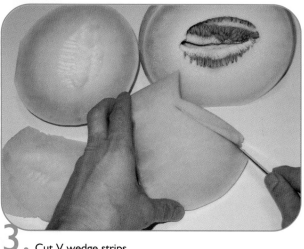

3. Cut V wedge strips.

6. Angle the bottoms.

4. Trim the tips of the shell round.

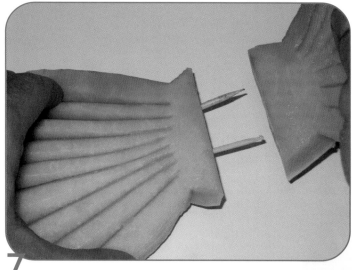

7. Push a wood pick half way in.

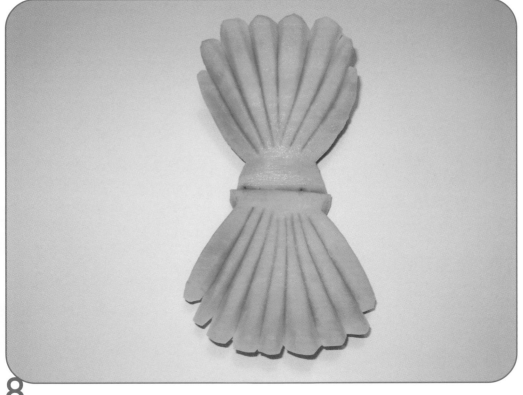

8. Attach shells.

9. Arrange a melon flower.

Carving Letters and Numbers

Uses: Platter Presentations, Personalized Centerpieces
Tools: French knife, vegetable knife, and paring knife

Tricks of the Trade

Use firm fruits and vegetables. Carvings can last up to a week. Soak carving pieces in water and lemon to revive. For ultimate control, work the knife like a jigsaw with short, quick jerks while pushing down with a light pressure. Use square wooden picks to attach pieces or break long wood skewers for more support. Draw subject on paper or use coloring book drawings as templates. Trace a design lightly onto the meat of the melon with the tip of the knife or tooth pick. The meat of the melon is always displayed out. All colors of the rind and meat can be part of the display.

Method

1. Place the melon on its side, facing you vertically.
2. Position the blade vertically across the side of the melon and cut a third slice off the side, **see fig. 1**. This piece is the base for this type of fruit carving; mix and match different melons for colors.
3. Position a template and transfer an image or draw on the meat side with the tip of a knife. For long, straight lines use the full blade of a French knife.
4. Grasp the product in one hand on a table, being careful not to damage the meat, and use a vegetable or a paring knife like a saw, **see fig. 2**.
5. Cut the sturdiest piece that holds the carving together last.
6. To add more dimension, trim off the face of the number deeper than the base, **see fig. 3, 4, 5, 6**.
7. Utilize the whole knife blade to cut long, straight V channels horizontally across the letter.
8. Cut V channels diagonally across the base, vertically and horizontally across the letter face with a paring knife.
9. Soak in lemon water if used more than once.
10. Use sturdy wooden picks or skewers to connect, support, and suspend sculpture.
11. To display, cut an orange in half, put half in a champagne glass flat side up, and attach letter with picks.

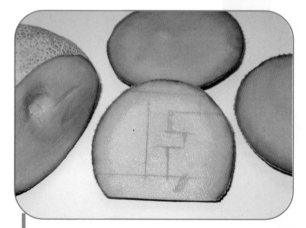

1. Cut three equal sides.

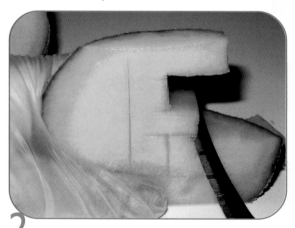

2. Trace and cut out figure.

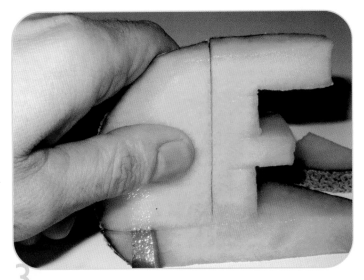

3. Cut the sturdiest piece last.

4. Square off the base.

5. Trim the letter's face.

6. Trim the base less.

*Uses: Platter Presentations,
Personalized Centerpieces*
*Tools: French knife, vegetable knife, and
paring knife*

Tricks of the Trade

By using firm fruits and vegetables, carvings can last up to a week. Soak carving pieces in water and lemon to revive them after the initial use. Always work the knife like a jigsaw with short, quick jerks and light pressure for ultimate control. Use square wooden picks to attach pieces or break long wood skewers for more support. Draw the subject to be carved on paper or use coloring book drawings as templates. Trace a design lightly onto the meat of the melon with the tip of the knife or tooth pick. The meat of the melon is always displayed out. All colors of the rind and meat can be part of the display. Poke a pilot hole into the melon rind before attaching a piece. From the basic designs illustrated here, many elaborate variations can be easily created.

Method

1. Place the melon on a table with the length pointing towards you.
2. Lay the blade vertically across the side of the melon and cut a third slice off the side.
3. Position a template and transfer an image or draw on the meat side with the tip of a knife, **see fig. 1, 2**.
4. Grasp the wing in one hand on a table and use a vegetable or a paring knife like a saw to carve.
5. Utilize the tip of the blade to cut curved V slices to resemble feathers and trim the tips, **see fig. 3, 4**.
6. To cut out body, angle up to start tail. When reaching the point where the tail meets the body, turn the blade so it curves down and continue down to the center of the belly. Begin to turn the blade up to meet the neck, then turn the blade down for the head, and back up for the beak. Trim all square edges round, **see fig. 5, 6**.
7. To connect the carvings, make a pilot hole in one piece and insert a wood pick or skewer into the other piece. Then attach and add more picks if needed to secure.
8. Insert picks into the back of each wing and attach to the rind side of the body.
9. Insert picks into the back of the bird and attach to the stand.
10. Soak in lemon water if used more than once.
11. Use sturdy wooden picks or skewers to connect, support, and suspend the sculpture, **see fig. 9**.

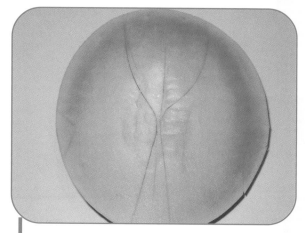

1. Trace a wing pattern.

2. Cut and trim wings.

3. Cut V's with the tip of the knife.

4. Trim the wing tips.

5. Cut the body outline deep.

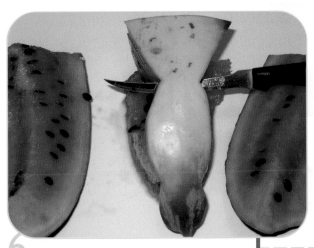

6. Trim the tail, belly, and head.

7. Trim the beak and round the edges out.

8. Push a pick in half way.

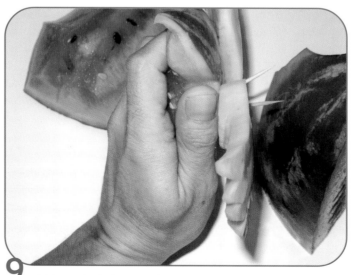

9. Make a pilot hole to attach the wings to the body and the completed bird to a base.

Carving Fish and Seaweed

Uses: *Platter Presentations, Personalized Centerpieces*
Tools: *French knife, vegetable knife, and paring knife*

Tricks of the Trade

Use firm fruits and vegetables and carvings can last up to a week. Soak carving pieces in water and lemon to revive.

Always work the knife like a jigsaw with short, quick jerks and light pressure for ultimate control. Use square wooden picks to make pilot holes and attach pieces or break long wood skewers for more support. Draw the subject on paper or use coloring book drawings as templates. Trace a design lightly onto the meat of the melon with a tip of the knife or tooth pick. All colors of the rind and meat can be part of the display. From the basic designs illustrated here, many elaborate variations can be easily created.

Fish Method

1. Cut and trim a square piece of watermelon rind with a half inch of meat still attached.
2. Trace the form of a sunfish lightly with the knife tip and cut out the form, **see fig. 1**.
3. Using the knife tip, outline the body of the fish about a quarter inch deep.
4. Lay the blade horizontal and cut through the fin to meet the previous cut, **see fig. 2**.
5. Round off edge around body, **see fig. 4**.
6. Work on a table. With the tip of the knife, cut a shallow V strip along the length of the fin, **see fig. 3**.
7. Use a small cap to cut an eye.
8. Make a pilot hole in the back of the fish to position on skewers, **see fig. 5**.

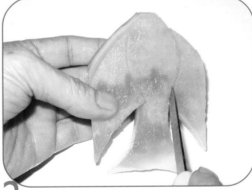

2. Cut in one quarter inch to outline the body.

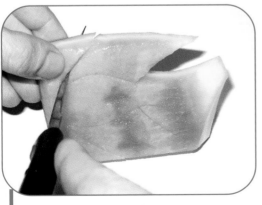

1. Trace and trim a sunfish form.

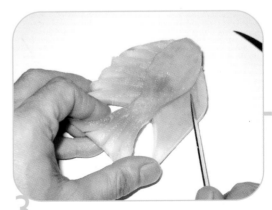

3. Cut a slice off the fin to meet the previous cut.

4. Round out the square edges.

5. Poke a pilot hole into the sculpture.

6. Insert a thick skewer into the base; attach the fish.

Leaf Method

1. Cut a wedge of melon and cut off most of the meat.
2. Work on a table. With the tip of the knife, cut a shallow V strip along the center length, letting the blade cut deep on the edge of the leaf, **see fig. 1, 2**.
3. Continue cutting V strips on both sides, **see fig. 3**.
4. Insert a wood pick in the bottom of the leaf to connect to the base.

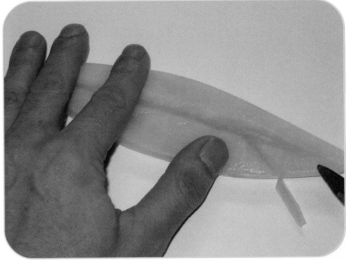

Figure 2.

Figure 1.

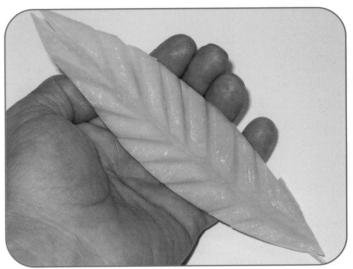

Figure 3.

Peel and Section Citrus

1. Cut off each end and position blade.

2. Saw knife along the curve of the orange.

3. Cut where the white meets the orange.

4. Slice along the side of the vein.

6. Remove section and fold over the vein.

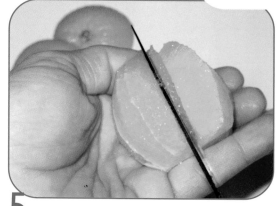

5. Slice along the other side.

Sliced Fruit Presentation

This Classical Display is comprised of one honeydew, one and a half each pineapple and cantaloupe. Always angle rows. Never arrange in straight lines and alternate colors for the best effect.

Method

1. First you should "tourney" the fruit, which is a method to peel and shape fruits and vegetables. You are trying to form 6 to 8 equal, smooth sides; with practice you will cut one side in one motion.
2. Cut off each end and stand it on end. Lay the knife on top, angled slightly away from product.
3. Use the knife like a saw and gently apply pressure while following the curve of the melon.
4. Turn the melon to position it. Now there is a guideline to follow; it's where the rind meets the meat.
5. Continue around the melon. Cut directly in half and deseed, being careful not to scoop the meat.
6. Place the flat side down, being careful not to damage the flat side.
7. See the Knife Handling instructions and proceed to slice the melon into quarter inch slices.
8. To fan out, place the palms of your hands on opposite corners and gently push them together.

Peeling and Slicing Melons

Uses: Platter Presentations and Food Holders
Tools: Sharp slicing knife or French knife

Tricks of the Trade

Beginners use the knife like a saw with quick, jerking motion. Pick out solid melons that are ripe but not soft. Check by tapping and squeezing on all sides. A good melon should be firm and sound solid for this method, so slices will stand up. If the melon sounds "hollow," it is too ripe for this particular use. Blemishes and discoloration are okay. Keep the tip of the blade pointed down with the handle pointing up when cutting. After the melon is peeled, stand it on the cut end and gently squeeze all sides to determine the firmest/thickest point. That point is where you want to cut through the length in the middle to make two halves. Seed the melon halves, being careful not to damage the meat. If the bottom walls of the halved melon are less than a half inch thick, the melon will not be useable for standing up the fanned slices. From the basic designs illustrated here, many elaborate variations can be easily created.

1. Cut each end level.

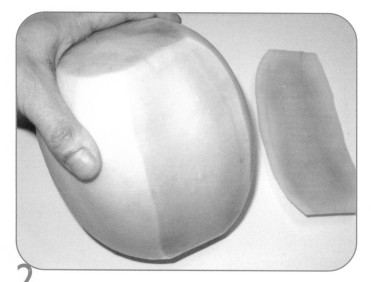

2. Follow the curve of the melon.

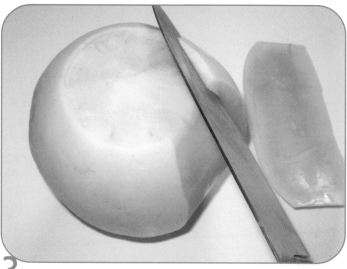

3. Note where the rind meets the meat.

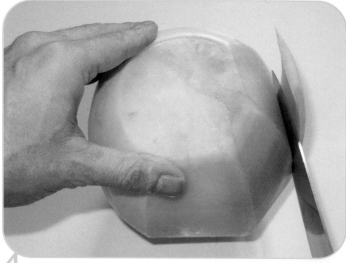

4. Use the knife like a saw.

5. Form six to eight equal sides.

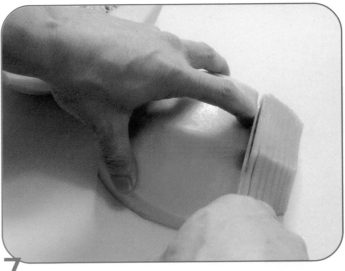

7. Slices are not sticking to the blade.

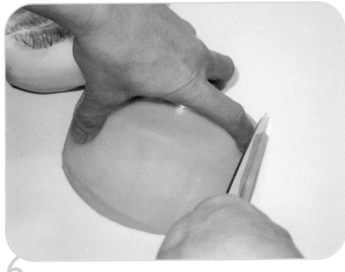

6. Keep the tip down and handle up.

8. Don't use any bad cuts.

Transfer melon to the platter before separating.

Gently squeeze the top right and bottom left corner.

Push the row of slices up to lengthen.

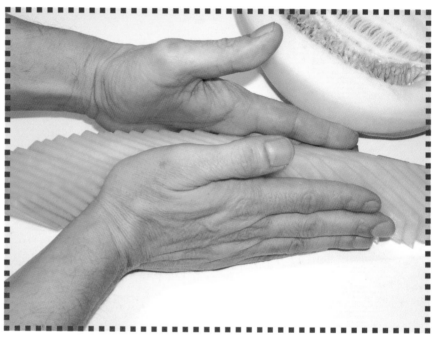

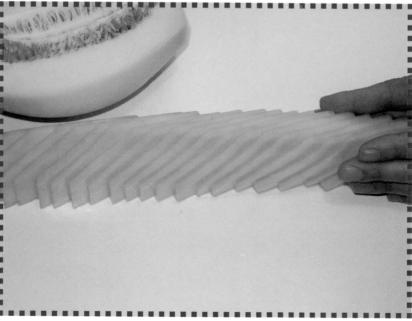

Make the slices separate evenly.

Fruit Presentation

Display is comprised of
3 cantaloupes, 2 pineapples,
1 pint strawberries,
1 pound of red grapes,
4 oranges,
and 2 limes.

1. Use a form to create a perfect circle.

2. Fan all rows in the same direction.

Discard any slices that fit incorrectly.

Display is comprised of a half watermelon, 3 cantaloupes, 3 pints strawberries, 1 honeydew, and 1 pineapple. Use any fruit centerpiece for displays; just be sure to place it on a riser for additional height. Risers can be anything, a soup bowl, a glass, or plastic ware. Just be sure to cover the riser with food.

Display is comprised of 2-1/2 cantaloupe, 1-1/2 pineapples, 1 honeydew, 3 oranges, 1 lime, 2 orange crowns, and a few red grapes. Utilize any type of fruits and berries in these basic designs.

Display is comprised of 2 pineapples, 2 honeydews, a half cantaloupe, 2 pints strawberries, a pound of red grapes, fresh parsley, and 2 orange crowns. Sliced fruit can be easily arranged into any symmetrical design, large or small.

The presentations are as endless as the variety of the produce market.

Masterpiece in Cheese

Cheese Displays

Uses: Platter Presentations
Tools: Sharp French knife and paring knife

Tricks of the Trade

Except for Swiss cheese, any cheese can be utilized (dice Swiss into inch thick cubes). Square, round, and tube-shaped cheeses are the best shapes for decorating platters. Wheels and ball cheese shapes are difficult to work with; square semi-soft is the best. When purchasing cheese, ask the deli to slice the cheese to your specifications. Clean your knife between cuts; if needed, even dip the knife in hot water to prevent sticking. From the basic designs illustrated here, many elaborate variations can be easily created.

Method

1. For a shingling effect, get the deli to slice the cheese into one quarter inch thick slices. No ends! For standing cheese slices up, slice the cheese into a little less than half inch thick slices.
2. Cut a five inch stack of sliced cheese through vertically across the middle of the stack.
3. Make a cross cut to divide into four equal stacks and cut corner to corner on each stack.
4. Finished products should be about one to two inches in size in any direction.
5. If product is larger, cut in the center again.
6. Handle like a deck of cards, *but don't shuffle*. Do not mix up the order in which they were cut.
7. Lay out in rows—with closer shingles, more cheese will be needed, and therefore, more people will be served.
8. Use a ruler or any object as a guide to make straight and curved rows. Position the ruler, then position the cheese against the side and remove, or draw a guideline with a damp finger.

1. Add height to a centerpiece with a riser.

2. Cover the pedestal and create a form with cubed cheese.

3. Use triangles to create a border.

4. Use the side of a knife to level the rows.

5. Contrast the colors of different cheeses.

6. Be sure everything is centered.

7. Lock in the row with standing triangles.

8. Use a lime with the ends cut off to raise lime crowns.

9. Garnish with orange, lime, and cantaloupe crowns.

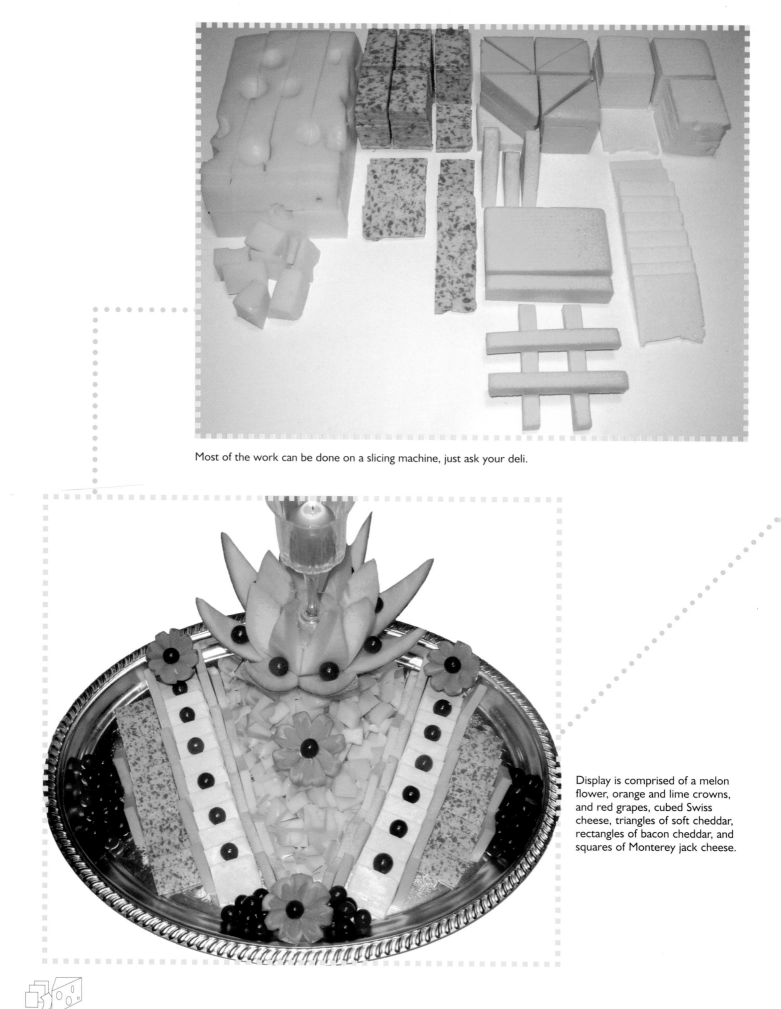

Most of the work can be done on a slicing machine, just ask your deli.

Display is comprised of a melon flower, orange and lime crowns, and red grapes, cubed Swiss cheese, triangles of soft cheddar, rectangles of bacon cheddar, and squares of Monterey jack cheese.

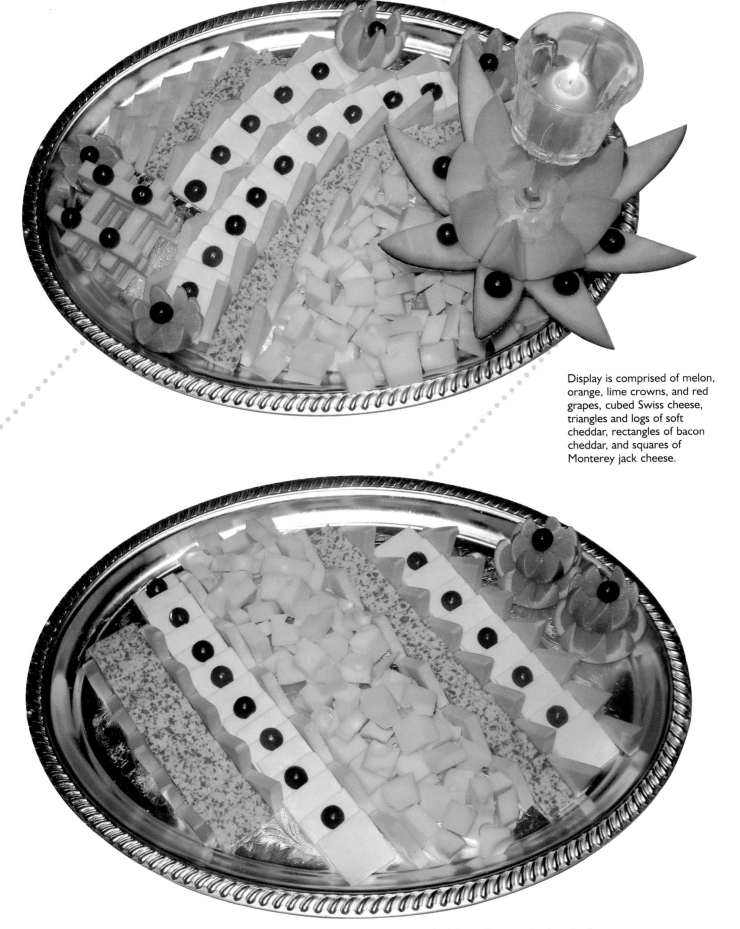

Display is comprised of melon, orange, lime crowns, and red grapes, cubed Swiss cheese, triangles and logs of soft cheddar, rectangles of bacon cheddar, and squares of Monterey jack cheese.

Display is comprised of orange and lime crowns and red grapes, cubed Swiss cheese, triangles of soft cheddar, rectangles of bacon cheddar, and squares of Monterey jack cheese.

Vegetables Appealing Displays

Vegetables Displays

Uses: Platter Presentations
Tools: Sharp French knife and paring knife

Tricks of the Trade

To refresh vegetables, soak them in tepid water the first time. The second time, refresh vegetables in cold water. The vegetable will swell, cuts will be more pronounced, and flowers will open. To prepare a day or two in advance, cover displays with damp cheesecloth and plastic wrap. Never show stems of any product; hide stems to give the impression of a growing plant. Use the Potato Daisy arrangement, Horn of Plenty, or bread dough sculpture for a backdrop. Use a whole tomato that has been leveled on the top and bottom as a riser to hold a tomato crown or tomato rose at a proper height. Don't forget, you always want to have a raised garnish to add dimension to the display. Never position all the products flat on the platter. From the basic designs illustrated here, many elaborate variations can be easily created.

To separate rows of vegetables, use a ruler or cardboard, placing it against the side of the first row, add a second row, and remove. Repeat the process.

Method

1. Select straight, fat cucumbers and evenly rounded tomatoes, and any other good quality produce.
2. Cut tops off tomatoes, turn upside down, and slice in the center to cut in half.
3. Cut each half into three or four even pieces. Use the standing wedges for various borders or rows (see the stand up wedge cutting material).
4. Cut a thin slice off the flattest side of a cucumber, position the cucumber on the flat side, and slice about a half inch thick, so the slices can be stood up and arranged in rows or arranged as a border to hold other vegetables in place. Don't forget to contrast the colors.
5. Cut various tulip flowers (see Vegetable Tulip material).
6. Cut broccoli florets: These florets should be put in arranged piles with all the stems faced down. Cauliflower is best quartered and sliced very thin; it looks good in a standing tomato border with a tomato rose in the center.
7. Black and green olives can be bordered with standing yellow squash slices, or cut the bottoms flat, stand the olives on end, and arrange into rows or borders. Cut small carrot sticks and push one in each black olive hole pointing up, or push a carrot stick through the olive for a garnish on an antipasto salad. Yellow squash can also be cut into tulips or wedge the squash by the length for a different appearance.
8. Cucumbers can also be carved into tulips or sliced paper thin and soaked in cold water overnight. Then take about six slices and form a cup. It's easy. Carrots, hicama, and diacon root are all good raw root vegetables to cut in sticks, slices or diamonds.

1. Position centerpiece.

2. Arrange broccoli with stems down.

3. Arrange standing tomato wedges.

4. Arrange a row of celery sticks.

5. Make a border with cucumber slices.

6. Fill in borders with vegetables.

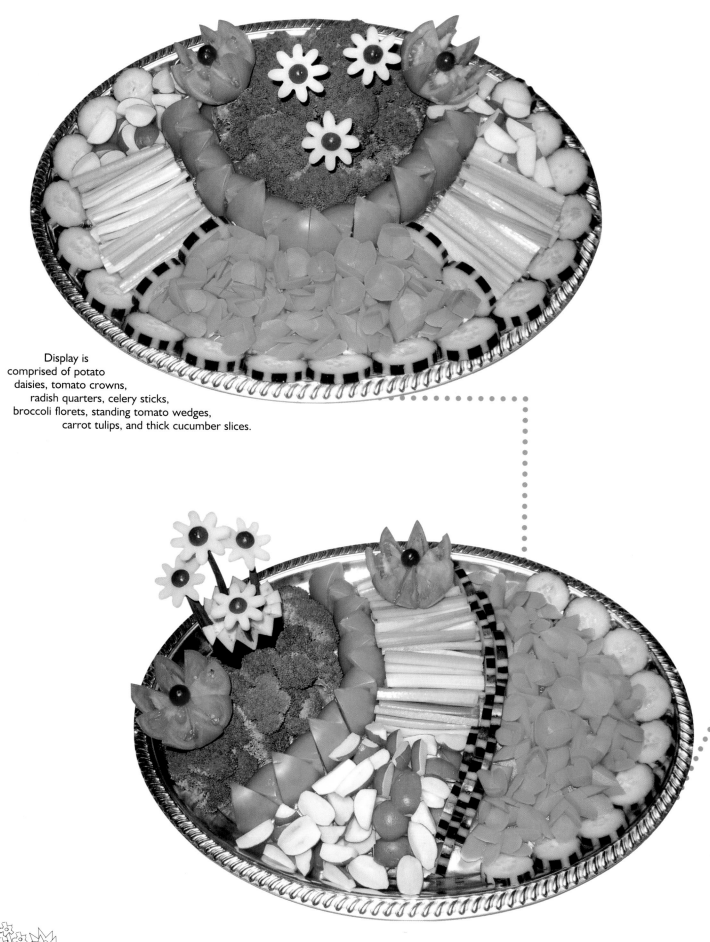

Display is
comprised of potato
daisies, tomato crowns,
radish quarters, celery sticks,
broccoli florets, standing tomato wedges,
carrot tulips, and thick cucumber slices.

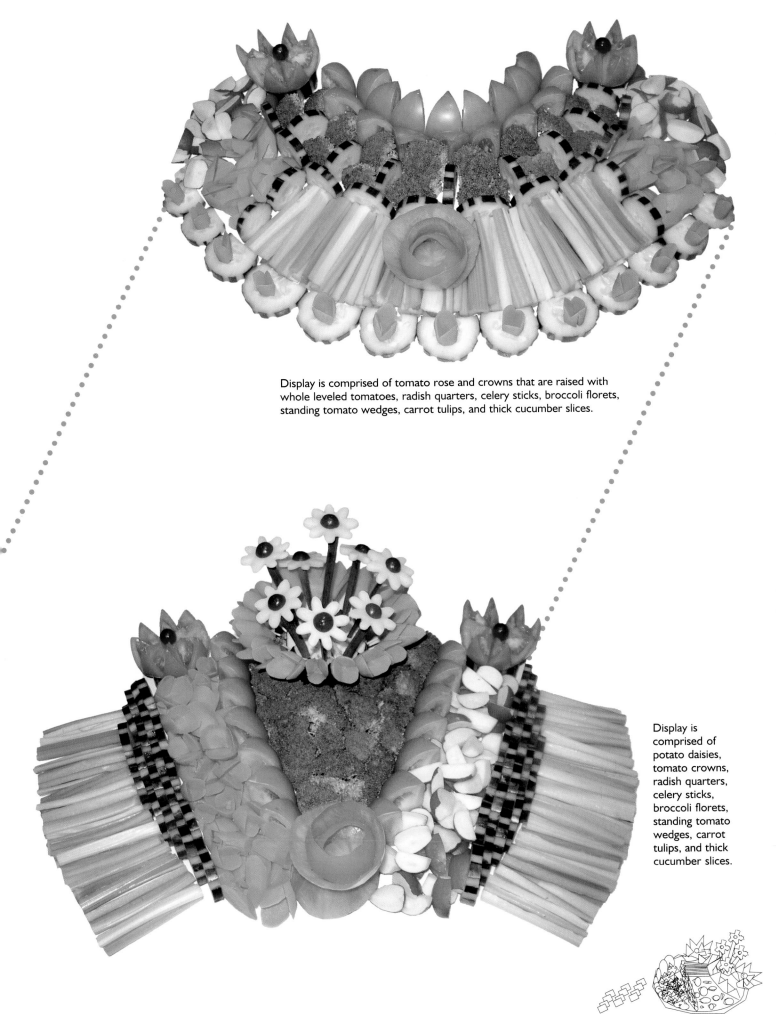

Display is comprised of tomato rose and crowns that are raised with whole leveled tomatoes, radish quarters, celery sticks, broccoli florets, standing tomato wedges, carrot tulips, and thick cucumber slices.

Display is comprised of potato daisies, tomato crowns, radish quarters, celery sticks, broccoli florets, standing tomato wedges, carrot tulips, and thick cucumber slices.

Deli Art Creations

Deli Art Displays

Uses: Platter Presentations
Tools: Sharp French knife and paring knife, latex gloves

Tricks of the Trade

Ask your local market's deli chef to slice meat thick enough to handle a whole, evenly cut slice without breaking. If you are going to fold slices over as illustrated, cut slices thicker still so the meat retains some shape and does not lay completely flat. The more uniform the slices are, the better the presentation will be.

From the checkout aisle to storage in your refrigerator, never put anything on top of packs of sliced meat or the slices will stick together. Wear latex gloves to handle deli meats. Prepare up to a day ahead of time, cover, and chill the platter thoroughly before serving.

When making a dome-shaped display for only a few people, use a filler such as a half head of lettuce. Use any torn or poorly cut deli slices for the bottom layer, while reserving the best looking slices to be displayed on top.

From the basic designs illustrated here, many elaborate variations can be easily created.

Method

1. Figure out a rough design that will incorporate all of the deli meats before you begin.
2. Shingled Ham: Fold in half and shingle slices to create rows, leaving the fold side exposed. The closer the shingles of meat are, the more meat it will take to complete a row. You can turn the rows in any direction. Put another layer on top of the first and another if it is needed.
3. Decorate by cutting thin, round slices of cucumber, squash, or tomato, cut in half and position flat side against the fold of the meat and/or insert a carrot or celery stick into the fold, leaving some of the stick exposed.
4. Turkey should be cut a little thicker and the big deli breasts should be cut in half by length to make half slices.
5. To create a dome of turkey with two pounds or more, mark a circle on the platter and fill this circle with half of the slices. Shingle the best you can in a circle, and fill the center with a small stack to form an evenly sided shape. Or simply layer a small bowl with shingled poorly cut slices, level the top, place a plate over the top of the

Display is comprised of a tomato rose, cherry tomato halves, yellow squash tulips, thick cucumber slices, carrot tulips, standing tomato wedges, celery sticks, salami, cured ham, and smoked turkey breast.

bowl, turn it over, and remove the bowl. Grasp the dome to slide it off the plate onto the serving platter. Then decorate the dome as illustrated with good slices. Position the first slice so the edge hangs from the dome's center top to the base.

6. Put the second slice at an angle that follows the curve of the dome and continue until you overlap the first five slices. Lift up those 5 slices and slide the end of the shingled slices under the beginning slices to form a continuous design. This method can also be used to interlock a circle.
7. To make a deli dome for less than fifteen people, cut the bottom off a head of iceberg lettuce. Use the head as the base to form a dome.
8. A saddle effect can be created with the same methods described for the turkey dome. Shape into a loaf.
9. To cover the top of the saddle, cut the bottoms off cherry tomatoes, garnish, and line them up.
10. Mass-production method: shingle flat slices back and forth in a straight row, creating a pyramid shape. Sliced cheese can also be displayed with this method or in stacks about 5 inches high with slices arranged in a star pattern. Just turn every other slice one quarter turn.

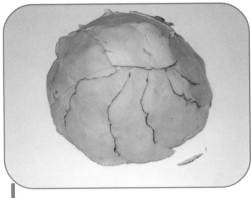

1. Stack and shingle slices to form a mound, saving the best-formed slices for last. Position these slices carefully, angling toward the top center and fanning out at the bottom. Circle the entire dome, overlapping a few slices from where you began.

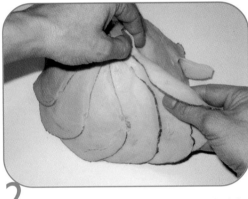

2. Lift the beginning slices, slide the end of the row under, and fold over to complete a row.

3. Shingle ham slices to follow the curve of the dome, border with tomato wedges and thick cut cucumber slices.

4. Shingle sliced folded salami (hold the preceding slice in place until the next slice is in position and continue until the circle is complete). Use a glass as a template.

5. Don't worry about making a perfect circle with the salami as you go. After the row is interlocked, adjust slices to reform the circle.

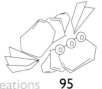

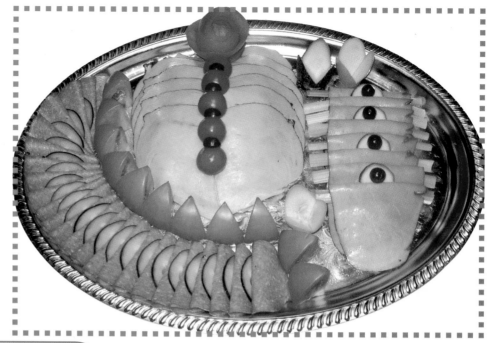

1. Position sliced deli meats.

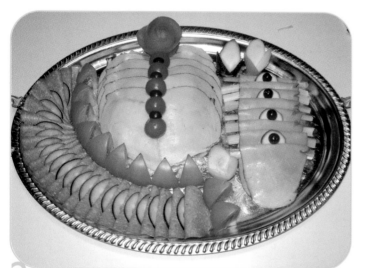

2. Garnish to cover the seams.

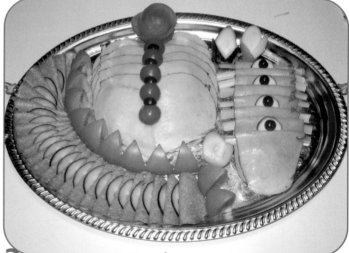

3. Be careful not to over decorate.

The garnish is comprised of a tomato rose, whole cherry tomatoes, thick cut half slices of cucumber, half slices of zucchini, cherry tomato halves, standing tomato wedges, and squash tulips.